CW00890270

THE ISLE OF PINES

Copyright © 2008 BiblioBazaar
All rights reserved

Original copyright: 1920

HENRY NEVILLE

THE ISLE OF PINES

An Essay in Bibliography by
Worthington Chauncey Ford

BIBLIOBAZAAR

THE ISLE OF PINES

TO
Charles Lemuel Nichols
lover of books
colleague
FRIEND

CONTENTS

PREFATORY NOTE.. 11

THE ISLE OF PINES 13
THE DOWSE COPIES 18
THE EUROPEAN EDITIONS 21
DUTCH EDITIONS... 23
FRENCH EDITIONS 25
ITALIAN EDITION 26
GERMAN EDITIONS... 27
THE S.G. NOT A CAMBRIDGE IMPRINT 30
THE COMBINED PARTS 33
THE PUBLISHERS... 35
NOT AN AMERICAN ITEM 36
THE AUTHOR 39
THE STORY.. 45
INTERPRETATIONS.. 47
DEFOE AND THE "ISLE OF PINES" 54

THE ISLE OF PINES, THE COMBINED
                    PARTS AS ISSUED IN 1668 55

PREFATORY NOTE

My curiosity on the "Isle of Pines" was aroused by the sale of a copy in London and New York in 1917, and was increased by the discovery of two distinct issues in the Dowse Library, in the Massachusetts Historical Society. As my material grew in bulk and the history of this hoax perpetrated in the seventeenth century developed, I thought it of sufficient interest to communicate an outline of the story to the Club of Odd Volumes, of Boston, October 23, 1918. The results of my investigations are more fully given in the present volume. I acknowledge my indebtedness to the essay of Max Hippe, "Eine vor-De-foesche Englische Robinsonade," published in Eugen Kölbing's "Englische Studien" xix. 66.

WORTHINGTON CHAUNCEY FORD
Boston, February, 1920

THE ISLE OF PINES

OR,

A late Discovery of a fourth ISLAND in Terra Australis, Incognita.

BEING

A True Relation of certain English persons, Who in the dayes of Queen Elizabeth making a Voyage to the East India, were cast-away, and wracked on the Island near to the Coast of Australis, and all drowned, except one Man and four Women, whereof one was a Negro. And now lately Ann Dom. 1667, A Dutch Ship driven by foul weather there, by chance have found their Posterity (speaking good English) to amount to ten or twelve thousand persons, as they suppose. The whole Relation follows, written, and left by the Man himself a little before his death, and declared to the Dutch by His Grandchild.

THE ISLE OF PINES

The scene opens in Cambridge, Massachusetts, in the year 1668, where in one of the college buildings a contest between two rival printers had been waged for some years. Marmaduke Johnson, a trained and experienced printer, to whose ability the Indian Bible is largely due, had ceased to be the printer of the corporation, or Society for the Propagation of the Gospel in New England, but still had a press and, what was better, a fresh outfit of type, sent over by the corporation and entrusted to the keeping of John Eliot, the Apostle. Samuel Green had become a printer, though without previous training, and was at this time printer to the college, a position of vantage against a rival, because it must have carried with it countenance from the authorities in Boston, and public printing then as now constituted an item to a press of some income and some perquisites. By seeking to marry Green's daughter before his English wife had ceased to be, Johnson had created a prejudice, public as well as private, against himself.[1]

1 Mass. Hist Soc. Proceedings, xx. 265.

Each wished to set up a press in Boston itself, but the General Court, probably for police reasons, had ordered that there should be no printing but at Cambridge, and that what was printed there should be approved by any two of four gentlemen appointed by the Court. It thus appeared that each printer possessed a certain superiority over his rival. In the matter of types Johnson was favored, as he had new types and was a trained printer; but these advantages were partially neutralized by indolence and by Green's better standing before the magistrates.[1]

In England the excesses of the printing-press during the civil war and commonwealth led to a somewhat strict though erratically applied censorship under the restoration. A publication must be licensed, and the Company of Stationers still sought, for reasons of profit, to control printers by regulating their production. The licensing agent in chief was a character of picturesque uncertainty and spasmodic action, Roger L'Estrange, half fanatic, half politician, half hack writer, in fact half in many respects and whole only in the resulting contradictions of purpose and performance. On one point he was strong—a desire to suppress unlicensed printing. So when in 1668 warrant was given to him to make search for unauthorized printing, he entered into the hunt with the zeal of a Loyola and the wishes of a Torquemada, harrying and rushing his prey and breathing threats of extreme rigor of fine, prison, pillory, and stake against the unfortunates who had neglected, in most cases because of the cost, to obtain the stamp of the licenser.[2]

New England was at this time England in little, with troubles of its own; but, having imitated the mother country in introducing supervision of the press, it also started in to investigate the printers of the colony, two in number, seeking to win a smile of approval from the foolish man on the throne. With due solemnity the inquisition was made. Green could show that all then passing through his press had been properly licensed.

1   See the chapters on Green and Johnson in Littlefield, The Early Massachusetts Press, 197, 209.

2   L'Estrange was called the "Devil's blood hound." Col. S. P., Dom. 1663-1664, 616.

Johnson, less fortunate, was caught with one unlicensed piece—"The Isle of Pines." A fine of five pounds was imposed upon him, as effectual in suppressing him as though it had been one of five thousand pounds. He could now turn with relish to two books then on his press, "Meditations on Death and Eternity" and the "Righteous Man's Evidence for Heaven;" for Massachusetts Bay, with its then powerful rule of divinity without religion, or religion without mercy, held out small hope of his meeting such a fine within the expedition of his natural life. But he made his submission, petitioned the General Court in properly repentant language, acknowledged his fault, his crime, and promised amendment[1] The fine was not collected, and the principal result of the incident was to further the very natural union of Johnson and Green, but with Johnson as the lesser member in importance.

No copy of Marmaduke Johnson's issue of the "Isle of Pines" has come to light in a period of 248 years. It might well be supposed that the authorities caught him before the tract had gone to press, and so snuffed it out completely. Our sapient bibliographers have dismissed the matter in rounded phrase: "'The Isle of Pines' was a small pamphlet of the Baron Munchausen order, which in its day passed through several editions in England and on the Continent,"[2] a description which would fit a hundred titles of the period. In July, 1917, Sotheby announced the sale of a portion of the Americana collected by "Bishop White Kennett (1660-1728) and given by

him to the Society for the Propagation of the Gospel in Foreign
Parts."

1   The petition it in Littlefield, i. 248.

2   Mats. Hist. Soc. Proceedings, xi. 247.

Lot No. 113 was described as follows:

[Neville (Henry)] The Isle of Pines, or a late Discovery of a
fourth Island in Terra Australis, Incognita, being a True Relation
of certain English persons who in the dayes of Queen Elizabeth,
making a Voyage to the East Indies, were cast away and wracked
upon the Island, wanting the frontispiece, head-line of title and
some pagination cut into, Bishop Kenneths signature on title. sm.
4to S. G. for Allen Banks, 1668.

The pamphlet was sold, I am told, for fourteen shillings,[1] and
resold shortly after to a New York bookseller for fifty-five dollars.
He was attracted by the imprint, which read in full, "London, by S.
G. for Allen Banks and Charles Harper at the Flower-Deluice near
Cripplegate Church." The general appearance of the pamphlet was
unlike even the moderately good issues of the English press, and the
"by S. G." not only did not answer to any London printer of the day,
except Sarah Griffin, "a printer in the Old Bailey,"[2] but was in form
and usage exactly what could be found on a number of the issues
of the press of Samuel Green, of Cambridge, Massachusetts.

1   The sale took place July 30, 1917.

2   Only once does her name occur in the Term Catalogues, when in February, 1673,
     the prints George Buchanan' Psalmorum Davidis Paraphrasis Poetica, which told
     for two shillings a copy. Samuel Gellibrand was not a printer but a bookseller, with
     a shop "at the Ball in St. Paul's Churchyard."

On comparing the first page of the text of his purchase with
the same page of an acknowledged London issue of the "Isle of
Pines" in the John Carter Brown Library,[1] the bookseller concluded
that the two were entirely different publications.

An expert cataloguer connected with one of the large auction
firms of New York then took up the subject. After a study of the
tract he became assured that it could only have been printed by

Samuel Green, of Cambridge, and he brought forward facts and comparisons which seemed conclusive and for which he deserves much credit. It was a clever bit of bibliographical work. With such an endorsement as to rarity and quality the pamphlet was again put to the test of the auction room. The cataloguer stated his case in sufficient fulness of detail and the first page of the text was reproduced.[2] Naturally the discovery sent a little thrill through the mad-house of bibliography. The tract was knocked down for $400 to a bookseller from Hartford, Connecticut, presumably for some local collection. The incident would have passed from memory had it not been for one of those accidents to which even the amateur bibliographer is liable.

1   No. 5 in the Bibliography, page 93, infra.

2   Nuggets of American History, American Art Association, November 19, 1917. The Isle of Pines was lot 142, and was introduced by the words, "Cambridge Press in New England." The catalogue was prepared by Mr. F. W. Coar.

In the bitter days of the winter of 1917-18 the working force of the Massachusetts Historical Society was contracted into one room—the Dowse Library—where was at least a semblance of warmth in the open fireplace.

THE DOWSE COPIES

One afternoon, when I had finished my work and the others had left, I picked up the catalogue of the Dowse Library and began idly to turn over its leaves. Incidentally, that catalogue is characteristic of the older methods of the Society. As is known to the elect, no book in the Dowse Library can ever leave the room in which it now rests, and of the catalogue twenty-five copies were printed and never circulated. If the library had been left in the Dowse house in Cambridgeport, its existence and contents could not have been more successfully hidden from the world. While reading the titles in a very casual way, my eye was caught by one which gave me a start. It read:

Sloetten (Cornelius van). The Isle of Pines; or a Late Discovery of a Fourth Island in Terra Australis Incognita. London, printed by G. S. for Allen Banks, 1668. With a New and Further Discovery of the Isle of Pines, 1668; and a duplicate of the Isle of Pines. 1 vol. small 4to, calf supr., gilt leaves. A most interesting, rare, and valuable work.

Even against the Editor of the Society the Dowse books are kept behind lock and key, though he is not under more than ordinary suspicion. So I was obliged to wait till the next day before my curiosity could be satisfied. I then found a thin volume, less than one-third of an inch in thickness, containing two copies of this very tract which the auction expert had identified as an issue of the "Isle of Pines" by Green, and a London issue of a second part of the "Isle of Pines," with the name of Cornelius Van Sloetten, as author. For more than fifty years this little volume had reposed in this well-known yet almost forgotten library, and no one had suspected or questioned the nature of its contents.

For full fifty years it had been in the care and at the call of Dr. Samuel A. Green, who claimed to be an expert on New England imprints of the seventeenth century, and one of the great wishes of whose life had been to establish his descent from this very printer, Samuel Green. Two copies within the same covers, of a tract long sought and of which only a single example had come to light in two centuries and a half—was not that alone something of a bibliographical coup?

I read two of the pieces—one of the Green issues and the second part as printed in England—making a few notes for future use. On returning to the matter some weeks later I found to my annoyance that every reference to the Green tract but one was wrong as to the page. Cold, haste, or weariness will account for a single or possibly two errors of reference, but to have a whole series—except one—go wrong pointed to failing eyes or mind. Very much put out, I read the tract a second time and corrected the page references, carefully checking up the result. Some days after I again took up the matter, and in verifying my first quotation found that I had again put down the wrong page number, and was surprised to find that the correct page was the one I had first given. This proved to be the case in all the references—except one. A book which could thus change its page numbering from week to week was bewitched—or I was careless. It occurred to me to compare the two copies of the tract as published by Green. The title-pages were exactly alike—not differing by so much as a fly speck, but one copy contained ten pages of text and the other only nine.

More than that, the general style and the types were quite different One was printed in a well-known broad but somewhat used type, such as could be seen in Green's printing, and the other in a finer font with much italic. There was no possibility of confusing the two issues. Only one conclusion was possible. I had in this volume the publication by Green, and the original issue by Marmaduke Johnson, but with Green's title-page. So for we seem to rest upon solid ground. It may be surmised that Green set up his "Isle of Pines" in rivalry to Johnson, but did not incur the discipline of the authorities; or that he had set it up and also took over Johnson's edition, using his own title-page; and in either case it is possible that a simple subterfuge, the imprint, "by S. G. for Allen Banks and Charles Harper," a London combination of publishers, caused the tract to escape the attention of the examining local censors. Here was another step in developing the history of this tract—the discovery of one of Johnson's issues, except for the title-page. So far as the American connection is concerned, it only remains to discover a Johnson issue with a Johnson title-page, for in his apology and submission to the General Court he states that he had "affixed" his name to the pamphlet.

THE EUROPEAN EDITIONS

The European connection is also not without interest, for the skit—the first part of the "Isle of Pines," published without name of author—had an extraordinary run.

In 1493 a little four-leaved translation into Latin of a Columbus letter announcing the discovery of islands in the west—De insulis nuper inventis—ran over Europe, startling the age by a simple relation which proved a marvellous tale as taken up by Vespuccius, Cortes, and a host of successors.[1] For a century the darkness of a new found continent slowly lifted and the record was collected in Ramusio, in De Bry, in Hulsius, and in Hakluyt, never felling treasuries of the wonderful, veritable schools for the adventurous. Another century had shown that, so fer from decreasing in greatness and in opportunities, the field of discovery had not begun to be tested, and in the summer of 1668 a new island—the Isle of Pines—was flashed before the London crowd, and proved that the flame of quest with danger was still burning. A new island! The interest was international, for nations had already long fought over the old discovered lands.

1   The intelligent industry of Mr. Wilberforce Eames has identified eleven issues of the letter of Columbus, printed in 1493, in Barcelona, Rome, Basle, Paris, and Antwerp; and twelve issues of the Novus Mundus of Vespucci us, printed in 1504, in Augsburg, Paris, Nuremberg, Cologne, Antwerp, and Venice. An earlier and even more extraordinary distribution of a letter of news is that of the letter purporting to be addressed by Prester John to the Emperor Manuel, which circulated through Europe about 1165. "How great was the popularity and diffusion of this letter," writes Sir Henry Yule, "may be judged in some degree from the fad that Zarncke in his treatise on Prester John gives a list of close on 100 mss. of it Of these there are eight in the British Museum, ten at Vienna, thirteen in the great Paris Library, and fifteen at Munich. There are also several renderings in old German verse." The cause of this popularity was the hope offered by the reported exploits of Prester John of a counterpoise to the Mohammedan power. Encyclopaedia Britannica, 11th ed., xxii. 305.

An even greater contest was being waged for commerce, and with the experience of Spain in gathering the precious metals from new found lands, every discovery of hitherto uncharted territory opened the possibility of wealth and an exchange of commodities, if rapine and piracy could not be practised. The merchant was an adventurer, and politics, quite as much as trade, controlled his movements; for the line between trader, buccaneer, and pirate faded away before conditions which made treaties of no importance and peaceful relations dependent upon an absence of the hope of gain. A state of war was not necessary to prepare the way for attack and plunder in those far distant oceans, and the merchantman sailed armed and ready to inflict as well as to repel aggression, only too willing to descend upon a weaker vessel or a helpless settlement of a power which had come to be regarded as a "natural enemy." So in Holland and in Germany the leaflets containing the story of the Isle of Pines were received with mingled feelings, exciting a desire to share in the possible benefits to be gained or extorted from natives of the new lands, or from those who had the first opportunity to exploit a virgin territory. On the first receipt of those leaflets merchants held back their vessels about to sail, to await more definite information on this fourth island of the Terra Australis incognita.

An examination of the known issues of the tract proves this interest and offers an almost unique study in bibliography; for I doubt if any publication made in the second half of the seventeenth century—even a state paper of importance, as a treaty—attained such speedy and widespread recognition. A list of the various issues will be found in an appendix: it only remains to call attention to a few of the many novelties and variant characteristics of the editions.

DUTCH EDITIONS

In June and July, 1668, four tracts on the Isle of Pines from the same pen were licensed and published in London, which may for convenience be designated the first and second parts of the narrative, and the two parts in continuation. From London the tract soon passed to Holland, which had ever been a greedy consumer of voyages of discovery, for the greatness of that nation depended upon the sea, at once its most potent enemy and friend.[1] Three Dutch editions have been found, the earliest in point of time being that made by Jacob Vinckel, of Amsterdam.

1   Holland was the centre of map publication as the twenty years before 1668 saw the issue of atlases by Jansson, Blaeu, Mercator, Doncker, Cellarius, Loon, Visscher, and Goos, all published at Amsterdam. Phillips' list for this period gives atlases published elsewhere—those of Boissevin (Paris, 1653), Lubin (Paris, 1659), Nicolosi (Rome, 1660), Dudley (Florence, 1661), Du Val (Paris, 1662), Jollain (Paris 1667), Cluver (Wolfen-büttel, 1667?) and Ortelius (Venice, 1667).

His second title is an exact translation of the second title of the London first part. This version, however, omitted an essential part of the relation. The London second title is also that of the issue made at Amsterdam by Jacob Stichter, being the Vinckel version, word for word, and almost line for line, but the type used is the gothic, and the spelling of words is not the same. Further, Stichter was possessed of some imagination and decorated his title-page with a map of a part of the island, showing ranges of hills, a harbor or mouth of a river, with conventional soundings, and two towns or settlements. As each of these issues contains only eight pages of text, the first London part only was known to the publishers. The third Dutch edition was put out by Joannes Naeranus, at Rotterdam, and in a foreword he gives the following reason for issuing the tract:

To the Reader A part of the present relation is also printed by Jacob Vinckel at Amsterdam, being defective in omitting one of the principal things, so do we give here a true copy which was sent to us authoritatively out of England, but in that language, in order that the curious reader may not be deceived by the poor translation, and for that reason this very astonishing history fall under suspicion. Lastly, admire God's wondrous guidance, and farewell.

His publication contains twenty pages of text, and is not an accurate translation of the English tract in parts, but rather a paraphrase of the text. To make the confusion the greater, he expressly states on the title-page that he used a copy received from London, and gives the London imprint which will fit only the first London part. For "by S. G." appears only on the title-page of that part.

FRENCH EDITIONS

From Amsterdam and under date July 19, 1668, a summary of the earlier Dutch issue with two paragraphs of introduction was sent to Paris, and was printed in a four-page pamphlet by Sébastien Marbre Cramoisy, the king's printer, whose name is so honorably connected with the Jesuit Relations—stories as remarkable as any offered in the "Isle of Pines" and of immeasurable value on the earliest years of recorded history in our New England. Even this summary, thus definitely dated, offers problems. The location of the island is given in general terms in the half-title as "below the equinoctial line," and in the text as in "xxviii or xxix degrees of Antartique latitude." Nowhere in the first London part is either location used, and in the second London part, which bears nearly the same date as the Cramoisy summary—July 22—twenty degrees of latitude is given. The writer of the summary thus allowed himself some freedom.

A second French edition, without imprint, contains eleven pages and is a translation of the first London part, paraphrased in sentences, but on the whole a close rendering of the English text There never was a title-page to this issue—the first page having the signature-mark A—yet with eleven pages only, it would seem fit that a title-page should round out the twelve for the convenience of printing.

ITALIAN EDITION

The Italian issue, made by Giacomo Didini, in Bologna and Venice, is a literal translation of Cramoisy's publication, and bears the same date, at Amsterdam, July 19, 1668. The original probably came from Paris, though it is possible that some Dutch merchant in Amsterdam sent a circular letter on the discovered Isle to his correspondents in Paris and Venice. It is unsafe to conjecture in such matters, for an Amsterdam issue may yet be found which will give, word for word, the French and Italian versions. Our ignorance on the press of the continent of those times, and especially the want of files of "corantos," or news sheets, close a wide field of research to the American inquirer. The catalogue of the British Museum gives 1669 as the probable year of issue. I see no good reason for rejecting 1668 as the more probable year. If the tract could go from London to Cambridge, in New England, in three months, it could pass from Amsterdam to Italy, by land or by sea, in an equal time.

GERMAN EDITIONS

From Holland the relation also penetrated the German states, finding ready welcome and arousing eager curiosity. Hippe regards the tract issued by Wilhelm Serlin, at Frankfort on the Main, as the first of the German publications, and, being translated from the Dutch, he shows that the translator used both the Amsterdam and the Rotterdam publications.[1] The Hamburg version claimed to be derived from the English original, but it followed closely the Serlin translation from the Dutch with modifications which might have been drawn from the London tract. An edition not mentioned by Hippe or identified by any bibliographer is in the John Carter Brown Library, and opens with the statement that it is translated from the English and not from the Dutch. It closely follows the text of the London first part. Very likely it is the edition found at Copenhagen, if the similarity of titles offers an indication of the contents. South Germany obtained its information from France, and while neither of the two issues avowedly translated from the French gives the place of publication, the fact that one is in Munich and the other in Strassburg offers some reason to conjecture that they came from the presses of those cities. The Munich issue is for the most part a summary of what was in the first London issue, and, if translated directly from a French version, must have been from one not now located, for it is different from those in the list in this volume. Of the Strassburg text, Hippe states that it follows the Rotterdam pamphlet Finally, at Breslau is what calls itself a complete publication of the combined parts from a copy obtained from London, but it is more probably based upon the Dutch translations printed in Amsterdam and Rotterdam, with additions drawn from the English.[2]

1   Hippe, 11.

On these German issues Hippe is full, but I have given only what is needed to identify them.

One of the strangest uses made of the narrative of Pine is to be found in Schoeben's translation into German of Jan Mocquet's "Voyages en Africque," etc., a work of some estimation which had already twice been published in France and once in a Dutch translation before Schoeben printed his edition in 1688. As pages inserted quite arbitrarily in Mocquets compilation, Schoeben gave Pine's story in full, with a paragraph of introduction which not a little abuses the truth while giving an additional color of truth. He asserted that while kept at Lisbon by the Dutch blockade, he was thrown much in the company of an Englishman, one of the Pine family, who were all regarded as notable seamen. From this man, then awaiting an opportunity to sail for the West Indies, our author heard a very strange story of the origin of the Pines, a story then quite notorious at Lisbon. Then follows, with some embroidery, a version of the Neville pamphlet, which is not like any German translation seen by me, but so full as to extend over ten pages of the volume. It ends with a reiteration of the wholly false manner in which this story had been obtained. So bold an appropriation of the narrative, with a provenience entirely new and as fictitious as the story itself, and its bodily inclusion by an editor in a work of recognized merit, where it is between two true recitals, cannot be defended.[1]

1   Mocquet's work originally appeared in Rouen in 1645, and a Dutch translation was published at Dordrecht in 1656. A second French issue, apparently unchanged in text, was put out at Rouen in 1665, and in 1618 Schoeben's edition, printed at Lüneberg by Johann Georg Lippers, preceded by eight years an English translation made by Nathaniel Pullen. The Pine tract appears, of course, only in Schoeben's volume.

The tract passed to Cambridge, Massachusetts, before or early in September, and it would indeed be interesting to know how and through whose hands it passed before reaching Marmaduke Johnson—to his undoing. Hezekiah Usher was the only bookseller in Boston at the time, and possibly his son, John, may have been associated with him. They ordered what they desired from London booksellers and publishers, and may have received voluntary consignments of publications from London. That would be a somewhat precarious venture, for nothing could be more different than the reading markets in Boston and in London, especially in the lighter products of the press. Had it come through the Ushers, the title-page might state that it had been printed "by M. J. for Hezekiah Usher," but in that event Usher would have suffered for not obtaining the needed license. The probability is that Johnson was alone responsible and was tempted by the hope of gain.

These were all contemporary issues, coming from the press within six months of the first appearance of the tract in London. So startling a popularity, so widely shown, was a tribute to the opportunity rather than to the contents of the piece. And the European interest continued for a full century. In Germany it was included in a number of collections of voyages, in Denmark it was printed in 1710 and 1789, and in France Abbé Prévost took it for his compilation of 1767 on discoveries. The English republication of 1778 has peculiar interest, for it was due to no other than Thomas Hollis, the benefactor of the library of Harvard College, who saw more in the tract than can now be recognized, and induced Cadell to reprint it.

THE S.G. NOT A CAMBRIDGE IMPRINT

In the absence of any positive objection, the conclusion of the auction expert—that the S. G. imprint was one of Samuel Green of Cambridge, Massachusetts—remained unquestioned. But a study of editions and of the chronological sequence of the English issues offers a decided negative to such a conclusion. The first part was licensed June 27, 1668. Van Sloetten dated the second part July 22, 1668, and the issue of the combined parts was licensed five days later, July 27. In the space of just four weeks all three trads were licensed, and the actual publication must have occurred within the same period of time. Such had been the start obtained by the first part that on the continent it was used for reprint and translation, almost to the neglect of the second part, and, as we have seen, most of these translations appeared before the end of 1668. Now the tract was not known in Massachusetts until discovered by the inquest on printers in September, and a S. G. or Samuel Green edition could hardly have come from the press before October, even if not delayed by the proceedings against Johnson. Yet on die title-page of the Dutch translation issued at Rotterdam in 1668, the printer states at length that it is from a copy from London, by S. G. for Allen Banks and Charles Harper, in the Lily near Cripplegate Church, and in his note "To the Reader" he expressly repeats that he obtained a copy of the work from London, in order to correct a faulty issue by another Dutch printer.

If S. G. was Samuel Green, we must suppose that one of his Cambridge issues was shipped to Rotterdam in time to be translated and reprinted before the end of the year. In point of time the thing could be done, but in point of probability it was impossible. Apart from his own statement, there were a thousand to one chances in favor of the Dutch printer obtaining the pamphlet from London;

there were ten thousand chances to one against his getting it from Massachusetts. I reject the supposition that this was a Cambridge imprint for that reason alone.

Additional evidence hostile to the claim may be adduced. The copy of the first tract in the British Museum is the S. G. for Banks and Harper.[1]

1   It is erroneously described as "an abridgment."

No other London imprint is to be found there or in the larger libraries of England. Of the three other copies located, that sold at audion (the White Kennett copy) and that in the Massachusetts Historical Society came direct from England, and the actual provenance of the copy in the New York Historical Society is not known. It belonged to Rufus King, long United States minister near the court of St James's, and is bound with other tracts under a general title of "Topographical Collection, Vol. I." The binding, Mr. Kelby tells me, is American. There is no mark to show when or where King obtained the pamphlet, and the Society did not receive it until 1906. That Rufus King belongs as much to Massachusetts as to New York is too slight a foundation on which to erect a claim that this particular tract was of Massachusetts origin.

In no case, therefore, can an American setting to any one of the four known copies of the S. G. "Isle of Pines" be established.[1] The probabilities are all against Samuel Green. The incident is a good example of the danger of giving play to the imagination on an appearance of a combination of fads cemented by interest.

Thus disappears from our memory the certain identification of the S. G. pamphlet as an early issue of the press in Cambridge, and with it goes my identification of the Johnson pamphlet with the S. G. title-page—a veritable pipe dream. It might be urged that as White Kennett was collecting on America, it would be more than probable that he would have had an American issue; but his own catalogue of 1713 describes the nine-page tract, and that is our London edition. I might claim still that my Johnson was a Johnson, with a London title-page; but the typographical adornment on the first page of its text is just the same as the adornment on the first page of the London issue—three rows of fleur-de-lys, thirty-seven in each row, and the same kind of type characters.[2]

1   Lowndes indexes it under George Pine, and describes a nine-page trait—probably
     the one now in the British Museum. He quotes a sale of a copy in it 60 (Puttkk) for
     £4.10s. He indexes the combined parts under Sloetten, and notes a copy, with the
     plate, sold in the White Knights sale for 1s.

2   To attempt to reason from types or rule of thumb measurements, however
     suggestive, leads to indefinite conclusions. For example, the width of the type
     page of the S. G. issue of the first part is exactly that of the English issue of the
     second part, but the former has 33 tines to the page and the latter a a. The width
     of the page in the variant S. G. issue is narrower and there are 38 and 39 lines to
     the page. But in the London second part the width of page varies by a quarter
     of an inch. We have Marmaduke Johnson's issue of Paine's Daily Meditations y
     issued in 1670 in connection with S. G. The ornamental border of fleur-de-lys is
     entirely different from those in the S. G. Isle of Pines. A copy of Johnson's issue
     of Scottow's translation of Bretz on the Anabaptists, printed in 1668, the very year
     of the Isle of Pines, shows a different foot of italics from that used in the Isle of
     Pines variant, yet the roman characters in the two pieces seem identical, and the
     width of page is exactly the same.

So I bid farewell to my theory, and can only congratulate myself on having cleared one point—the London issue—and on having introduced a new confusion by the discovery of a second London issue with an identical title-page, a problem for the future to solve. I much doubt if a true Johnson issue will ever be found, for I believe the action of the authorities prevented its birth.

In the library of Mr. Henry E. Huntington is a London issue of which I do not find another example. It contains sixteen pages, and the title-page gives neither printer's name nor place of publication. It may be the first issue, or it may be a later re-issue of the tract, for the type, especially the italic, is better than that in the S. G. issue. The punctuation also is more carefully looked after, and the whole appearance suggests an eighteenth century print. As the original was duly licensed, there was no reason to suppress the names of printer or booksellers. Nor could the contents of the piece call out controversy or hostility from any political faction or religious following. It was proper for the author to omit his name from the publication, if he desired to remain unknown; but the publisher, having the support of the licenser, had every reason to advertise his connexion with the tract, although he could not have anticipated so ready an acceptance by the public. While I place the Huntington pamphlet first in the bibliography, I am more inclined to regard it as a publication made at a later time.

THE COMBINED PARTS

The English edition of thirty-one pages in the John Carter Brown Library, with an engraved frontispiece,[1] offers still further proof that the S. G. issue was made in London. In place of being entirely different from the S. G. tract, it is precisely the same so far as text is concerned. For it is nothing more than the two parts combined, but combined in a peculiar manner. The second part was opened at page 6 and the first part inserted, entire and without change of text[2] This insertion runs into page 16, where a sentence is inserted to carry on the relation: "After the reading and delivering unto us a Coppy of this Relation, then proceeded he on in his discourse." The rest of the text of the second part follows, and pages 27-31 of the combined parts seem to be the very type pages of pages 20-24 of the second part[3] In this sandwich form one must read six pages before coming to the text of the first part, and a careless reader, comparing only the respective first pages, would conclude that a pamphlet of thirty-one pages could have no likeness to one of nine.

1   The plate in the copy in the John Carter Brown Library does not belong to that issue, but is inserted in so clumsy a manner as to prevent reproduction. The same plate is found in a copy of the ten-page S.G. issue in the library of Mr. Henry E. Huntington, and to all appearances belongs to that issue.

2   The last sentence on page 6 of the second part read: "Then proceeded he on in his discourse saying," and there are no pages numbered 7 and 8, although there is no break in the text, the catch-word on page 6 being the first word on page 9. In the combined parts, the last words on page 6 constitute a phrase: "which Copy hereafter followeth."

3   The only change made is in the heading of the Post-script, which was wrongly printed in the second part as "Post-script." On page 26 of the combined parts the words "except burning" were inserted, not appearing in the second part.

On typographical evidence it is safe to assume that the three pieces came from the same press, and to assert that the second part and the combined parts certainly did. The initials S. G. are found only on the first part.

THE PUBLISHERS

The imprints of the three parts agree that the booksellers or publishers handling the editions were Allen Banks and Charles Harper. The first part gives their shop as the "Flower-De-luice near Cripplegate Church," the second part as the "Flower-de-luce" as before, and the combined parts as "next door to the three Squerrills in Fleet-street, over against St. Dunstans Church." The church is still there, with more than two centuries of dirt and soot marking its walls since Neville wrote, and Chancery and Fettar Lanes enable one to place quite accurately the location of the booksellers' shop. Only three times do the names of Banks and Harper appear as partners on the Stationers' Registers,[1] and they separated about 1671, Banks going to the "St Peter at the West End of St Pauls." If any judgment may be drawn from their publications after ceasing to be partners, Banks leaned to light literature and may have been responsible for taking up the "Isle of Pines." Yet Harper was Neville's publisher in 1674 and in 1681, a fact which may indicate a personal relation.[2]

1   Eyre and Rivington, ii. 386, 388, and 410.

2   See page 34, infra.

NOT AN AMERICAN ITEM

By some curious chance this little pamphlet has come to be classed as Americana. Bishop Kenneth's Catalogue may have been the source of this error, leading collectors to believe that the item was a true relation of an actual voyage, and possibly touching upon some phase of American history or geography. The rarity of the pamphlet would not permit such a belief to be readily corrected. The existence also of two Isles of Pines in American waters may have aided the belief.

One of these islands is off the southwestern end of Cuba. On his second voyage, Columbus had sailed along the south coast of Cuba, and June 13,1494, reached an island, which he named Evangelista. Here he encountered such difficulties among the shoals that he determined to retrace his course to the eastward. But for that experience, he might have reached the mainland of America on that voyage. The conquest of the island of Cuba by Diego Velasquez in 1511 led to its exploration; but geographers could only slowly appreciate what the islands really meant, for they were as much misled by the reports of navigators as Columbus had been by his prejudice in favor of Cathay.

Toscanelli's map of the Atlantic Ocean (1474) gives many islands between Cape Verde and the "coast of spices," of which "Cippangu" is the largest and most important.[1]

1   This map, as reconstructed from Martin Behaim's globe, is in Scottish Geographical Magazine, 1893.

On Juan de laCosa's sea chart, 1500, Cuba is fairly drawn, with the sea to the south dotted with islands without names. In a few years the mist surrounding the new world had so far been dispelled as to disclose a quite accurate detail of the larger West Indian islands[1] and to offer a continent to the west, one that placed Cipangu still far too much to the east of the coast of Asia.[2] An island of some size off the southwest of Cuba seems to have been intended at first for Jamaica, but certainly as early as 1536 that island had passed to its true position on the maps, and the island to the west is without a name. Nor can it be confused with Yucatan, which for forty years was often drawn as an island. On the so-called Wolfenbuttel-Spanish map of 1525-30 occurs the name "J. de Pinos," probably the first occurrence of the name upon any map in the sixteenth century. Two other maps of that time—Colon's and Ribero's, dated respectively 1527 and 1529—call it "Y de Pinos," and on the globe of Ulpius, to which the year 1542 is assigned, "de Pinos" is clearly marked. Bellero's map, 1550, has an island "de pinolas." Naturally, map-makers were slow to adopt new names, and in the numerous editions of Ptolemy the label St Iago was retained almost to the end of the century.[3] On the Agnese map there are two islands, one named "S. Tiago," the other "pinos," which introduced a new confusion, though he was not followed by most geographers until Wytfliet, 1597, gave both names to the same island—"S. Iago siue Y de Pinas"—in which he is followed by Hondius, 1633.[4] Ortelius, 1579, adopts "I Pinnorum," while Linschoten, 1598, has "Pinas," and Herrera, 1601, "Pinos."

1   The Agnese Atlas of 1529 may be cited as an example.

2   See, for example, the so-called Stobnicza [Joannes, Stobnicensis] map of 151a, and the Ptolemy of 1513 (Strassburg).

3   Muenster, 1540. Cabot, 1544, and Desceller, 1546, give "Y de Pinos."

4   Mr. P. Lee Phillips, to whom I am indebted for references to atlases of the time, also supplies the following: Lafreri, 1575 (?) "S. Tiagoj" Percacchi, 1576, "S. Tiago;" Santa Cruz, 1541, "Ya de Pinosj" and Dudley, 1647, "I de Pinos." Hakloyt (iii. 617) prints a "Ruttier" for the West Indies, without date, but probably of the end of the sixteenth century, which contains the following; "The markes of Isla de Pinos. The Island of Pinos stretcheth it selfe East and West, and is full of homocks, and if you chance to see it at full sea, it will shew like 3 Islands, as though there were divers soundes betweene them, and that in the midst is the greatest; and in rowing with them, it will make all a firme lande: and upon the East side of these three homocks it will shewe all ragged; and on the West side of them will appeare unto you a lowe point even with the sea, and oftentimes you shall see the trees before you shall discerne the point."

When the name given by Columbus was dropped and by whom the island was named "de Pinos" cannot be determined.

Our colleague, Mr. Francis R. Hart, has called my attention to a second Isle of Pines in American waters, being near Golden Island, which was situated in the harbor or bay on which the Scot Darien expedition made its settlement of New Edinburgh. The bay is still known as Caledonia Bay, and the harbor as Porto Escoces, but the Isla de Pinas as well as a river of the same name do not appear on maps of the region. The curious may find references to the island in the printed accounts of the unfortunate Darien colony.

The Isle of Pines could thus be found on the map as an actual island in the West Indies; but the "Isle of Pines" of our tract existed only in the imagination of the writer. The mere fact of its having been printed—but not published—in Cambridge, Massachusetts, does not entitle it to be classed even indirectly as Americana, any more than Bunyan's Pilgrim's Progress or Thomas à Kempis could be so marked on the strength of their having a Massachusetts imprint Curiosities of the American press they may be, but they serve only as crude measures of the existing taste for literature since become recognized as classic.

The dignified Calendar of State Papers in the Public Record Office, London, gravely indexes a casual reference to the tract under West Indies, and the impression that the author wrote of the Cuban island probably accounts for the different editions in the John Carter Brown Library, as well as for the price obtained for the White Kennett copy. No possible reason can be found, however, for regarding the "Isle of Pines" in any of its forms as Americana.

THE AUTHOR

Thus far I have been concerned with externals, and before turning to the contents of the tract itself in an endeavor to explain the extraordinary popularity it enjoyed, something must be said of the author—Henry Neville. Like most of the characters engaged in the politics of England in the middle of the seventeenth century, he has suffered at the hands of his biographer, Anthony à Wood,[1] merely because he belonged to the opposite party—the crudest possible measure of merit For the odium politicum and the odium theologicum are twin agents of detraction, and the writing of history would be dull indeed were it not for the joy of digging out an approximation to the truth from opposing opinions. Where the material is so scanty it will be safer to summarize what is known, without attempting to pass finally upon Neville's position among his contemporaries.

1   Athenæ Oxonienses (Bliss), iv. 413.

The second son of Sir Henry Neville, and grandson of Sir Henry Neville (1564?-1615), courtier and diplomatist under Elizabeth and James I, Henry Neville was born in Billing-bear, Berkshire, in 1620. He became a commoner of Merton College in 1635, and soon after migrated to University College, where he passed some years but took no degree. He travelled on the continent, becoming familiar with modern languages and men, and returned to England in 1645, to recruit for Abingdon for the parliament Wood states that Neville "was very great with Harry Marten, Tho. Chaloner, Tho. Scot, Jam. Harrington and other zealous commonwealths men." His association with them probably arose from his membership of the council of state (1651), and also from his agreement with them in their suspicions of Cromwell, who, in his opinion, "gaped after the government by a single person." In consequence he was banished from London in 1654, and on Oliver's death was returned to parliament December 30,1658, as burgess for Reading. An attempt to exclude him on charges of atheism and blasphemy failed.

He was undoubtedly somewhat closely associated with James Harrington, the author of "Oceana," and was regarded as a "strong doctrinaire republican." He was a member of the club—the Rota—formed by Harrington for discussing and disseminating his political views, a club which continued in existence only a few months, from November, 1659, to February, 1660; but its name is embalmed in one of Harrington's essays—"The Rota"—published in 1660, and extracted from his "Art of Law-giving," which was itself an abridgment of the "Oceana."

At this time, says Wood, Neville was "esteemed to be a man of good parts, yet of a factious and turbulent spirit." On the restoration he "sculk'd for a time," and, arrested for a supposed connection in the Yorkshire rising of 1663, he was released for want of evidence against him, retiring from all participation in politics. For twenty years before his death he lived in lodgings in Silver Street, near Bloomsbury market, and dying on September 20, 1694, he was buried in the parish church of Warfield, Berkshire. By his wife, Elizabeth, daughter of Richard Staverton of Warfield, he had no issue.[2] In his retirement he found occupation in political theory. He translated some of the writings of Machiavelli, which he had obtained in Italy in 1645, and published some verses of little merit.

1   Wood.

2   Dictionary of National Biography, XL. 259.

It cannot be said that a reading of Neville's productions before 1681 raises him in our estimation, it certainly does not give the impression of a man of letters, a student of government, or even a politician of the day. There is always the possibility in these casual writings of a purpose deeper than appears to the reader of the present day, of a meaning which escapes him because the special combination of events creating the occasion cannot be reconstructed. The "Parliament of Ladies," which was published in two parts in 1647, has little meaning to the reader, though they appeared in the year when the Parliament took notice of the "many Seditious, False and Scandalous Papers and Pamphlets daily printed and published in and about the cities of London and Westminster, and thence dispersed into all parts of this Realm, and other parts beyond the Seas, to the great abuse and prejudice of the People, and insufferable reproach of the proceedings of the Parliament and their Army."[1]

To write, print, or sell any unlicensed matter whatsoever would be liable to fine or imprisonment, and to whet the zeal of discovery one-half of the fine was to go to the informer. Every publication, from a book to a broadsheet, must bear the name of author, printer, and licenser. Neither of Neville's pamphlets of 1647 conformed to the requirements of this act, which is not, however, positive evidence that they did not appear after the promulgation of the law. Suppression of printing has proved a difficult task to rulers, even when supported by public opinion or an army. The Stationers' Registers show that the "Parliament of Ladies" and its sequel were not properly entered; nor do they contain any reference to Neville's "News from the New Exchange," issued in 1650.[2]

Nine years passed before he printed a pamphlet which marked his break with Cromwell—"Shuffling, Cutting, and Dealing in a Game of Picquet."[3]

1   Acts and Ordinances of the Interregnum, i. 1021. Though dated September 30, the act was entered at Stationers' Hall September 19. Eyre and Rivington, i. 276.

2   It was reprinted in 1731.

3   It is in the Harleian Miscellany, v. 298, and a copy of the meanly printed original is in the Ticknor Collection, Boston Public Library.

This little pamphlet was put out in the poorest dress possible, bespeaking a press of meagre equipment, and a printer without an idea of the form which even the leaflet can assume in skilful hands. Without imprint, author's name, or any mark of identification, it indicates a secret impression and issue—one of the many occasional pamphlets which appeared at the time from "underground" shops which least of all wanted to be known as the agent of publication. Neville either avowed the authorship or it was traced to him, and the displeasure of Cromwell and banishment from London followed.

In 1681 he printed "Discourses concerning Government," which was much admired by Hobbes, and even Wood admits that it was "very much bought up by the members [of parliament], and admired: But soon after, when they understood who the author was (for his name was not set to the book), many of the honest party rejected, and had no opinion of it" A later writer describes it as an "un-Platonic dialogue developing a scheme for the exercise of the royal prerogative through councils of state responsible to Parliament, and of which a third part should retire every year."[1] Reissued at the time under its better known title—"Plato Redivivus"[2]—it was reprinted in 1742,[3] and again by Thomas Hollis in 1763.

1   Dictionary of National Biography, XL. 259.

2   Plato Redivivus, or A Dialogue concerning Government: wherein, by Observations drawn from other Kingdoms and States both ancient and modern, an Endeavour is used to discover the politick Distemper of our own; with the Causes and Remedies. The Second Edition, with Additions. In Octavo. Price 2s. 6d. Printed for S. I. and sold by R. Dew. The Term Catalogues (Arber), 1.443—the issue for May, 1681. The initials S. I. do not again occur in the Catalogues, and R. Dew is credited with only two issues, both in May, 1681, neither giving the location of his shop. The tract called out several replies, such as the anonymous Antidotum Brittanicum and Goddard's Plato's Demon, or the State Physician Unmasked (1684).

3   A copy is in the Library Company, Philadelphia.

His translations from Machiavelli are not so easily traced, nor is any explanation possible for his having delayed for nearly thirty years publication of evidence of his admiration for the Florentine politician. He was not alone in desiring to make the Italian political moralist better known, for translations of the "Discourses" and "The Prince," with "some marginal animadversions noting and taxing his [Machiavelli's] errors," by E. D.[1] was published in a second edition in November, 1673, but I do not connect Neville with that issue. In the following year the connection of Charles Harper's name with the "Florentine History" suggests Neville, as does a more ambitious undertaking of the "Works," first fathered by another London bookseller, but with which Harper was concerned in 1681:

The Florentine History, in Eight Books. Written by Nicholas Machiavel, Citizen and Secretary of Florence: now exactly translated from the Italian. In Octavo. Price, bound, 6s. Printed for Charles

Harper, and J. Amery, at the Flower de luce, and Peacock, in Fleet street.[2]

The Works of the Famous Nicholas Machiavel, Citizen and Secretary of Florence. Containing, 1. The History of Florence. 2. The Prince. 3. The Original of the Guelf and Ghibilin Factions. 4. The life of Castrucio Castraceni. 5. The murther of Vitelli, etc., by Duke Valentine. 6. The State of France. 7. The State of Germany. 8. The Discourses of Titus Livius. 9. The Art of War. 10. The Marriage of Belphegery a Novel.[3]

1   Edward Dacres.

2   The Term Catalogues (Arber i. 18—the issue for November 25,1674.) It was entered at Stationers' Hall, June 20, 1674, "under the hands of Master Roger L'Estrange and Master Warden Mean" with the statement that the translation was made by "J. D. Gent."

3   This novel wa added by Starker to a translation of novels by Gomez deQueverdoy Villegas published in November, 1670. The name of the printer suggests a connection with Neville.

11. Nicholas Machiavel's Letter in Vindication of himself and his Writings. All written originally in Italian; and from thence newly and faithfully Translated in English. In Folio. Price, bound, 18s. Printed for J. Starkey at the Mitre in Flret street near Temple Bar.

[Same Title.] The Second Edition. Printed for J. Starkey, C. Harper, and J. Amery, at the Miter, the Flower de luce, and the Peacock, in Flret street. Folio. Price, bound, 16s.[1]

1   The Term Catalogues (Arber) i.199—the issue for February, 1675. Entered at Stationers' Hall, February 4, 1674-75, "under the hands of Master Roger L'Estrange and Master Warden Roycroft," with the statement that the translation was made by "J.B. Salvo iure cuilibet." The resort to L'Estrange in both instances is suggestive. 2 Ib 453—the issue for June, 1681. "The Works of that famous Nicholas Machiavel" is announced in the Catalogues, June, 1675, for publication by R. Boulter, in Cornhill, and at the same price of 18s., but I doubt if Neville had anything to do with that translation.

It may be admitted that questions of government were eagerly discussed in the seventeenth century. It was only needed to live under the Stuarts and to pass through the Civil War and Protectorate to realize that a transition from the divinely anointed ruler to a self-constituted governor resting upon an army, and again to a trial of the legitimate holder of royal prerogative, offered an education in matters of political rule which naturally led to a constitutional monarchy, and which could not be equalled in degree or lasting importance until the American colonies of Great Britain questioned the policy of the mother country toward her all too energetic children. Hobbes' "Leviathan, or the Matter, Form and Power of a Commonwealth, Ecclesiastical and Civil," appeared in 1651, a powerful argument for absolutism, but cast in such a form as to make the writer an unwelcome adherent to royalty in exile.

In 1652 Filmer published his "Observations concerning the Original of Government," one of a series of tracts, completed by his "Patriarcha," printed after his death, which has made him a prophet of the extreme supporters of the divine origin of kingship. These are only examples of the political discussion of the day, and to them may be added Harrington, whose "Oceanan" appeared in 1656.[1] It satisfied no party or faction, and a second edition was not called for until 1700, when other writings of the author were added. This compilation was, in 1737, pirated by a Dublin printer, R. Reilly, who added Neville's "Plato Redivivus;"[2] but the third English edition (1747), issued by the same printer who made the second edition, omitted Neville's tract.

1   Entered at Stationers' Hall by Livewell Chapman, September 19,1656. Eyre and Rivington, ii. 86.

2   Bibliotheca Liudeusianat ii. 4228.

THE STORY

"The Isle of Pines" was Neville's fifth publication, issued nine years after his fourth, a political tract: "Shuffling, Cutting and Dealing in a Game of Picquet" Like most titles of the day, that of "The Isle of Pines" did not fail in quantity. It was repeated word for word, except the imprint, on the first page of the text. Briefly, the relation purports to have been written by an Englishman, George Pine, who at the age of twenty shipped as book-keeper in the India Merchant, which sailed for the East Indies in 1569.

Having rounded the Cape of Good Hope and being almost within sight of St. Lawrence's Island, now Madagascar,[1] they encountered a great storm of wind, which separated the ship from her consorts, blew many days, and finally wrecked the vessel on a rocky island. The entire company was drowned except Pine, the daughter of his master, two maid-servants, and one negro female slave. They gathered what they could of the wreckage, and Pine and his companions lived there in community life, a free-love settlement By the four women he had forty-seven children, and in his sixtieth year he claimed to have 565 children, grandchildren, and great-grandchildren. It was from one of his grandchildren that the Dutch ship received the relation. Apart from the title-page, the entire tract is occupied by the story of George Pine, from whom the island took its name. In 1667, or ninety-eight years after Pine was wrecked, the Dutch captain estimated that the population of the island amounted to ten or twelve thousand persons. Methuselah, with his years to plead for him, might boast of such breeding, but in ordinary man it is too near the verminous, the rat, the guinea-pig, and the rabbit, to be pleasant.

1   It was the Island of St. Laurence of James Lancaster's Voyage, 1593. Hakluyt, Principall Navigations, vi. 401.

The publication must have attracted attention at once, for before the end of July Neville put forth a second part, "A New and further Discovery of The Isle of Pines," which purported to be the relation of the Dutch captain to whom the history of Pines had been confided. It is an unadorned story such as might have been gathered from a dozen tales in Hakluyt or Purchas, and is interesting only in giving the name of the Dutch captain—Cornelius Van Sloetton—and the location of the supposed island—longitude 76° and latitude 20°, under the third climate—which places it to the northeast of Madagascar. Almost immediately after the publication of the second part it was combined with the first part, as already described, and published late in July or early in August Cornelius Van Sloetton, as he signed himself in the second part, became Henry Cornelius Van Sloetten in the combined issue.

INTERPRETATIONS

It was Pine's relation which received the greatest attention on the continent, and that was chiefly concerned in describing his performances in populating the island. It was therefore with only a mild surprise that I read in one of those repulsively thorough studies which only a German can make, a study made in 1668 of this very tract, "The Isle of Pines," the assertion that Pines, masquerading as the name of the discoverer and patriarch of the island, and accepted as the name of the island itself, was only an anagram on the male organ of generation—penis. On one of the German issues in the John Carter Brown Library this has also been noted by a contemporary hand.[1] Such an interpretation reduces our tract to a screaming farce, but it closely suits the general tone of other of Neville's writings, which are redolent of the sensual license of the restoration. To this I would add an emendation of my own. The name adopted by Neville was Henry Cornelius van Sloetten. It suggests a somewhat forcible English word—slut—of doubtful origin, although forms having some resemblance in sound and sense occur in the Scandinavian languages.

1   Christian Weise, Prof. Polit, in augusteo in A. 1685.

Such interpretations seem to fit the work better than that of a German critic, who sees in the book a sort of Utopia, a model community, or an exhibition in the development of law and order. Free love led to license, maids were ravished, and the complete promiscuity of intercourse disgusted Pine, who sought to suppress it by force and, in killing the leader of a revolt, a man with negro blood in his veins, to impose punishments for acts which he had himself done. The ground for believing that Neville had any such purpose when he wrote the book is too slight to be accepted. In 1668 the author had no call to convey a lesson in government to his countrymen by any means so frankly vulgar and pointless as the "Isle of Pines." If Neville had intended such a political object, a phrase would have sufficed to indicate it. No such key can be found in the text, and there is nothing to show that, politician as he was, he realized that such an intimation could be drawn from his paragraphs.

To assume, therefore, that so carefully hidden a suggestion of a model republic could have aided the circulation of the pamphlet at the time, or at any later period, is to introduce an element unnecessary to explain the vogue of the relation. It passed simply as a story of adventure, and as such it fell upon a time when a wide public was receptive to the point of being easily duped. Wood asserts that the "Isle of Pines," when first published, "was look'd upon as a mere sham or piece of drollery; "[1] and there are few contemporary references to the relation of either Pine or Van Sloetten, and those few are of little moment If the seamen, who were in a position to point out discrepancies of fad in the story, made any comment or criticism, I have failed to discover them.

[1]   Athenæ Oxoniensis (Bliss), iv. 410.

Neville himself freely played with the subject, and it is strange that he did not excite some suspicion of his veracity among his readers. He had told in his first part of a Dutch ship which was driven by foul weather to the island and of the giving to the Dutch the story of Pine. His second part is the story of the Dutch captain, sailing from Amsterdam, re-discovering the Isle of Pines, and returning home—that is, to Holland. Yet Neville for the combined issue, and presumably only a few days after giving out the first part, composed two letters from a merchant of Amsterdam—Abraham Keek—dated June 29 and July 6, saying that the last post from Rochelle brought intelligence of a French vessel which had just arrived and reported the discovery of this very island, but placing it some two or three hundred leagues "Northwest from Cape Finis Terre," though, he added with reasonable caution, "it may be that there may be some mistake in the number of the Leagues, as also of the exact point of the compass from Cape Finis Terre."

Keek offered an additional piece of geographical information, that "some English here suppose it maybe the Island of Brasile which have been so oft sought for, Southwest from Ireland."[1] The first letter of Keek is dated five days after the licensing of the first part of the "Isle of Pines," and the second sixteen days before the date of Sloetten's narrative. It is hardly possible that Neville could have been forgetful of his having made a Dutch vessel responsible for the discovery and history of Pine, and it is more than probable that he took this means of giving greater verisimilitude to the Isle of Pines, by bringing forward an independent discovery by a French vessel. However intended, the ruse did not contribute to such a purpose, as the combined parts did not enjoy as wide a circulation as the first part.

1   See page 53, infra.

On the continent a German, who knew the tract only as translated into German through a Dutch version of the English text, and therefore imperfectly, gave it serious consideration, and had little difficulty in finding inconsistencies and contradictions. Some of his questions went to the root of the matter. It was a Dutch ship which first found the Isle of Pines and its colony; why was not the discovery first announced by the Dutch? Piece by piece the critic takes down the somewhat clumsily fashioned structure of Neville's fiction, and in the end little remains untouched by suspicion. No such examination, dull and labored in form, and offering no trace of imagination which wisely permits itself to be deceived in details in order to be free to accept a whole, could pass beyond the narrow circle of a university.

As an antidote to the attractions of Neville's tract it was powerless, and to-day it remains as much of a curiosity as it was in 1668, when it was written. Indeed, a question might be raised as to which tract was less intentionally a joke—Neville's "Isle of Pines," or our German's ponderous essay upon it? At least the scientific ignorance of the Englishman, perfectly evident from the start, is more entertaining than the pseudo-science of the German critic, who boldly asserts as impossible what has come to be a commonplace.[1]

1   Das verdachtige Pineser-Eylandd, No. 29 in the Bibliography. It it dedicated to Anthonio Goldbeck, Burgomaster of Altona, and the letter of dedication b dated at Hamburg, October 26, 1668.

Hippe calls attention to the geography of the relation as not the least interesting of its features, for the neighborhood of the Island of Madagascar was used in other sea stories as a place of storm and catastrophe. "The ship on which Simplicissimus wished to return to Portugal, suffered shipwreck likewise near Madagascar, and the paradisiac island on which Grimmelshausen permits his hero finally to land in company with a carpenter, is also to be sought in this region. In precisely the same way the shipwreck of Sadeur,[1] the hero of a French Robinson Crusoe story, happens on the coast of Madagascar, and from this was he driven in a southerly direction to the coast of the southern land."

1   La Terre Australe commue, a romance written by Gabriel de Foigny (pseud. J. Sadeur), describing the stay of Sadeur on the southern continent for more than thirty-five years, The original edition, made in Geneva in 1676, is said to contain "many impious and licentious passages which were omitted in the later editions." Sabin (xviii. 220) gives a list of editions, the first English translation appearing in 1693. It is possible that the author owed the idea of his work to Neville's pamphlet.

In most of the older surveys of the known world America counts as the fourth part, naturally coming after Europe, Asia, and Africa. Even that arrangement was not generally accepted. Joannes Leo (Hasan Ibn Muhammad, al-Wazzan), writing in 1556, properly called Africa "la tierce Partie du Monde;" but the Seigneur de la Popellinière, in his "Les Trois Mondes," published in 1582, divided the globe into three parts—1. Europe, Asia, and Africa; 2. America, and 3. Australia. A half century later, Pierre d'Avitz, of Toumon (Ardèche), entitled one of his compositions "Description Générale de l'Amérique troisiesme partie du Monde," first published in 1637.[2] The expedition under Alvaro de Mendana de Nevra, setting sail from Callao, November 19, 1567, and steering westward, sought to clear doubt concerning a continent which report had pictured as being somewhere in the Pacific Ocean. The Solomon Islands rewarded the enterprise, and with New Guinea and the Philippines completed a connection between Peru and the continent of Asia. There had long existed, however, a settled belief in the existence of a great continent in the southern hemisphere, which should serve as a counterpoise to the known lands in the northern.

1   A copy is in the Boston Athenaeum.

The geographical ideas of the times required such a continent, and even before the circumnavigation of Africa, the world-maps indicated to the southward "terra incognita secundum Ptolemeum,"[1] or a land of extreme temperature and wholly unknown.[2] The sailing of ships round the Cape of Good Hope dissipated in some degree this belief but it merely placed some distance between that cape and the supposed Terra Australis which was now extended to the south of America, separated on the maps from that continent only by the narrow Straits of Magellan, and stretching to the westward, almost approaching New Guinea.[3]

1   As on the Ptolemy, Ulm, 1482.

2   As in Macrobius, In Sommium Scipionis Expositio, Brescia, 1483. 3 See the map of Oronce Fine, 1522, and Ortelius, Orbis Terrarum 1592. 4 The "Quiri Regio" was long marked on maps as a continent lying to the south of the Solomon Islands.

3   This was first republished at Augsburg in 1611; in a Latin translation in Henry Hudson's Descriptio ac Delimeatis, Amsterdam, 1612, in Dutch, Verhael van seher Memorial, Amsterdam, 1612; in Bry, 1613, and shortly after in Hulsius; in French, Paris, 1617; and in English, London, 1617. I give this list because even so interesting an announcement of a genuine voyage did not have so quick an acceptance as Neville's tract with almost the same title.

Such an expanse of undiscovered land, believed to be rich in gold, awakened the resolution of Pedro Fernandez de Queiros, who had been a pilot in the Mendafia voyage of 1606. By chance he failed in his object, and deceived by the apparent continuous coast line presented to his view by the islands of the New Hebrides group, he gave it the resounding name of Austrialia del Espiritu Santo, because of the King's title of Austria. On the publication of his "Relation" at Seville in 1610, the name was altered, and he claimed to have discovered the "fourth part of the world, called Terra Australis incognita." Seven years later, in 1617, it was published in London under the title, "Terra Australia incognita, or A new Southerne Discoverie, containing a fifth part of the World." It is obvious that geographers and their source of information— the adventurous sea captains—were not agreed upon the proper number to be assigned to the Terra Australis in the world scheme. Even in 1663 the Church seemed in doubt, for a father writes "Mémoires touchant l'établissement d'une Mission Chrestienne dans la troisième Monde, autrement apellé la Terre Australe,

Méridionale, Antartique, & I connue."[1] That Neville even drew his title from any of these publications cannot be asserted, nor do they explain his designation of the Isle of Pines as the fourth island in this southern land; but they show the common meaning attached to Terra Australis incognita, and his use of the words was a clever, even if not an intentional appeal to the curiosity then so active on continents yet to be discovered.

1   Printed at Paris by Claude Cramoisy, 1663. A copy is in the John Carter Brown Library. In 1756 Charles de Brosse published his Histoire des Navigations aux Terres Australes from Vespuccius to his own day, which was largely used by John Callender in compiling his Terra Australis Cogmta, 1766-68.

Another volume, however, written by one who afterwards became Bishop of Norwich, may have been responsible for the conception of Neville's pamphlet. This was Joseph Hall's "Mundus Alter et Idem sive Terra Australis ante hac semper incognita longis itineribus peregrini Academici nuperrime lustrata." The title says it was printed at Frankfort, and the statement has been too readily accepted as the fact, for the tract was entered at Stationers' Hall by John Porter, June 2, 1605, and again on August 1, 1608.[1] The biographer of Bishop Hall states that it was published at Frankfort by a friend, in 1605, and republished at Hanau in 1607, and in a translated form in London about 1608. It is more than probable that all three issues were made in London, and that the so-called Hanau edition was that entered in 1608. On January 18, 1608-09, Thomas Thorpe entered the translation, with the address to the reader signed John Healey, who was the translator.[2] This carried the title: "The Discovery of a New World, or a Description of the South Indies hitherto unknown."[3] It is a satirical work with no pretense of touching upon realities. Hallam wrote of it: "I can only produce two books by English authors in this first part of the seventeenth century which fall properly under the class of novels or romances; and of these one is written in Latin. This is the Mundus Alter and Idem of Bishop Hall, an imitation of the later and weaker volumes of Rabelais. A country in Terra Australis is divided into four regions, Crapulia, Virginia, Moronea, and Lavernia. Maps of the whole land and of particular regions are given; and the nature of the satire, not much of which has any especial reference to England, may easily be collected. It is not a very successful effort."[4]

1   Stationers' Registers (Arber), in. 291, 386.

2   Ib. 400. Healey made an "exceptionally bad" translation of St. Augustine's De
     Civitate Dei, which remained the only English translation of that work until
     1871.

3   In the Bodleian Library is a copy of the translation with the title, The Discovery of
     a New World, Tenterbelly, Sheeland, and Fooliana, London, n.d.

4   Introduction to the Literature of Europe, 2d éd., II. 167.

While a later critic, Canon Perry, says of it: "This strange composition, sometimes erroneously described as a 'political romance,' to which it bears no resemblance whatever, is a moral satire in prose, with a strong undercurrent of bitter jibes at the Romish church, and its eccentricities, which sufficiently betray the author's main purpose in writing it. It shows considerable imagination, wit, and skill in latinity, but it has not enough of verisimilitude to make it an effective satire, and does not always avoid scurrility."[1] Like Neville's production, the satire was misinterpreted.

The title of Neville's tract also recalls the lost play of Thomas Nash—"The Isle of Dogs"—for which he was imprisoned on its appearance in 1597, and suffered, as he asserted, for the indiscretion of others. "As Actaeon was worried by his own hounds," wrote Francis Meres in his "Palladis Tamia," "so is Tom Nash of his Isle of Dogs." And three years later, in 1600, Nash referred in his "Summers Last Will" to the excitement raised by his suppressed play. "Here's a coil about dogs without wit! If I had thought the ship of fools would have stay'd to take in fresh water at the Isle of Dogs, I would have furnish'd it with a whole kennel of collections to the purpose." The incident was long remembered. Nine years after Nash's experience John Day published his "Isle of Gulls," drawn from Sir Philip Sidney's "Arcadia."[2]

1   Dictionary of National Biography, xxiv. 76.

2   I take these facts from Sir Sidney Lee's sketch of Nash in the Dictionary of
     National Biography, XL. 107.

DEFOE AND THE "ISLE OF PINES"

I would apologize for taking so much time on a nine-page hoax did it not offer something positive in the history of English literature. It has long been recognized as one of the more than possible sources of Defoe's "Robinson Crusoe." It is truly said that the elements of a masterpiece exist for years before they become embodied, that they are floating in the air, as it were, awaiting the master workman who can make that use which gives to them permanent interest Life on an island, entirely separated from the rest of mankind, had formed an incident in many tales, but Neville's is believed to have been the first employment by an English author of island life for the whole story. And while Defoe excludes the most important feature of Neville's tract—woman—from his "Robinson Crusoe," issued in April, 1719, he too, four months after, published the "Further Adventures of Robinson Crusoe," in which woman has a share. It would be wearisome to undertake a comparison of incident; suffice it to say that the "Isle of Pines" has been accepted as a pre-Defoe romance, to which the far greater Englishman may have been indebted.

THE ISLE OF PINES, THE COMBINED PARTS AS ISSUED IN 1668

The Isle of Pines

OR,

A late Discovery of a fourth ISLAND near Terra Australis, Incognita

BY

Henry Cornelius Van Sloetten.

Wherein is contained.

A True Relation of certain English persons, who in Queen Elizabeths time, making a Voyage to the East Indies were cast away, and wracked near to the Coast of Terra Australis, Incognita, and all drowned, except one Man and four Women. And now lately Anno Dom. 1667. a Dutch Ship making a Voyage to the East Indies, driven by foul weather there, by chance have found their Posterity, (speaking good English) to amount (as they suppose) to ten or twelve thousand persons. The whole Relation (written and left by the Man himself a little before his death, and delivered to the Dutch by his Grandchild) Is here annexed with the Longitude and Latitude of the Island, the situation and felicity thereof, with other matter observable.

Licensed July 27. 1668.

London, Printed for Allen Banks and Charles Harper next door to the three Squerrills in Fleet-Street, over against St Dunstans Church, 1668.

Two Letters concerning the Island of Pines to a Credible person in Covent Garden.

IT is written by the last Post from Rochel, to a Merchant in this City, that there was a French ship arrived, the Mailer and Company of which reports, that about 2 or 300 Leagues Northwest from Cape Finis Terre, they fell in with an Island, where they went on shore, and found about 2000 English people without cloathes, only some small coverings about their middle, and that they related to them, that at their first coming to this Island (which was in Queen Elizabeths time) they were but five in number men and women, being cast on shore by distress or otherwise, and had there remained ever since, without having any correspondence with any other people, or any ship coming to them. This story seems very fabulous, yet the Letter is come to a known Merchant, and from a good hand in France, so that I thought fit to mention it, it may be that there may be some mistake in the number of the Leagues, as also of the exact point of the Compass, from Cape Finis Terre; I shall enquire more particularly about it. Some English here suppose it may be the Island of Brasile which have been so oft sought for, Southwest from Ireland, if true, we shall hear further about it; your friend and Brother, Abraham Keek.

Amsterdam, July the 6th 1668.

IT is said that the Ship that discovered the Island, of which I hinted to you in my last, is departed from Rochel, on her way to Zealand, several persons here have writ thither to enquire for the said Vessel, to know the truth of this business. I was promised a Copy of the Letter Amsterdam, June the 29th 1668, that came from France, advising the discovery of the Island above-said, but its not yet come to my hand; when it cometh, or any further news about this Island, I shall acquaint you with it,

Your Friend and Brother,
A. Keck.

Discovered Near to the Coast of Terra Australis Incognita, by Henry Cornelius Van Sloetten, in a Letter to a friend in London, declaring the truth of his Voyage to the East Indies.

SIR,

I Received your Letter of this second instant, wherein you desire me to give you a further account concerning the Land of Pines, on which we were driven by distress of Weather the last Summer, I also perused the Printed Book thereof you sent me, the Copy of which was surreptiously taken out of my hands, else should I have given you a more fuller account upon what occasion we came thither, how we were entertained, with some other circumstances of note wherein that relation is defective. To satisfie therefore your desires, I shall briefly yet sully give you a particular account thereof, with a true Copy of the Relation itself; desiring you to bear with my blunt Phrases, as being more a Seaman then a Scholler.

April the 26th 1667. We set sail from Amsterdam, intending for the East-Indies; our ship had to name the place from whence we came, the Amsterdam burthen 350. Tun, and having a fair gale of Wind, on the 27 of May following we had a sight of the high Peak Tenriffe belonging to the Canaries, we have touched at the Island Palma, but having endeavoured it twice, and finding the winds contrary, we steered on our course by the Isles of Cape Ferd, or Insula Capitis Viridis, where at St. James's we took in fresh water, with some few Goats, and Hens, wherewith that Island doth plentifully abound.

June the 14. we had a sight of Madagascar, or the Island of St Laurence, an Island of 4000 miles in compass, and scituate under the Southern Tropick; thither we steered our course, and trafficked with the inhabitants for Knives, Beads, Glasses and the like, having in exchange thereof Cloves and Silver. Departing from thence we were incountred with a violent storm, and the winds holding contrary, for the space of a fortnight, brought us back almost as far as the Isle Del Principe; during which time many of our men fell sick, and some dyed, but at the end of that time it pleased God the wind favoured us again, and we steered on our course merrily, for the space of ten days: when on a sudden we were encountered with such a violent storm, as if all the four winds together had conspired for our destruction, so that the stoutest spirit of us all quailed, expecting every hour to be devoured by that merciless element of water, sixteen dayes together did this storm continue, though not with such violence as at the first, the Weather being so dark all the while, and the Sea so rough, that we knew not in what place we were, at length all on a sudden the Wind ceased, and the Air cleared, the Clouds were all dispersed, and a very serene Sky followed, for which we gave hearty thanks to the Almighty, it being beyond our expectation that we should have escaped the violence of that storm.

At length one of our men mounting the Main-mast espyed fire, an evident sign of some Countrey near adjoyning, which presently after we apparently discovered, and steering our course more nigher, we saw several persons promiscuously running about the shore, as it were wondering and admiring at what they saw: Being now near to the Land, we manned out our long Boat with ten persons, who approaching the shore, asked them in our Dutch Tongue What Eyland is dit? to which they returned this Answer in English, "that they knew not what we said." One of our Company named Jeremiah Hanzen who understood English very well, hearing their words discourst to them in their own Language; so that in fine we were very kindly invited on shore, great numbers of them flocking about us, admiring at our Cloaths which we did wear, as we on the other side did to find in such a strange place, so many that could speak English and yet to go naked.

Four of our men returning back in the long Boat to our Ships company, could hardly make them believe the truth of what they had seen and heard, but when we had brought our ship into harbour, you would have blest your self to see how the naked Islanders flocked unto us, so wondering at our ship, as if it had been the greatest miracle of Nature in whole World.

We were very courteously entertained by them, presenting us with such food as that Countrey afforded, which indeed was not to be despised; we eat of the Flesh both of Beasts, and Fowls, which they had cleanly drest, though with no great curiosity, as wanting materials, wherewithal to do it; and for bread we had the inside or Kernel of a great Nut as big as an Apple, which was very wholsome, and found for the body, and tasted to the Pallat very delicious.

Having refreshed our selves, they invited us to the Pallace of their Prince or chief Ruler, some two miles distant off from the place where we landed; which we found to be about the bigness of one of our ordinary village houses, it was supported with rough unhewn pieces of Timber, and covered very artificially with boughs, so that it would keep out the greatest showers of Rain, the sides thereof were adorned with several forts of Flowers, which the fragrant fields there do yield in great variety. The Prince himself (whose name was William Pine the Grandchild of George Pine that was first on shore in this Island) came to his Pallace door and saluted us very courteously, for though he had nothing of Majesty in him, yet had he a courteous noble and deboneyre spirit, wherewith your English Nation (especially those of the Gentry) are very much indued.

Scarce had he done saluting us when his Lady or Wife, came likewise forth of their House or Pallace, attended on by two Maid-servants, the was a woman of an exquisite beauty, and had on her head as it were a Chaplet of Flowers, which being intermixt with several variety of colours became her admirably. Her privities were hid with some pieces of old Garments, the Relicts of those Cloaths (I suppose) of them which first came hither, and yet being adorned with Flowers those very rags seemeth beautiful; and indeed modesty so far prevaileth over all the Female Sex of that Island, that with grass and flowers interwoven and made strong by the peelings of young Elms (which grow there in great plenty) they do plant together so many of them as serve to cover those parts which nature would have hidden.

We carried him as a present some few Knives, of which we thought they had great need, an Ax or Hatchet to fell Wood, which was very acceptable unto him, the Old one which was cast on shore at the first, and the only one that they ever had, being now so quite blunt and dulled, that it would not cut at all, some few other things we also gave him, which he very thankfully accepted, inviting us into his House or Pallace, and causing us to sit down with him, where we refreshed our selves again, with some more Countrey viands which were no other then such we tasted of before; Prince and peasant here faring alike, nor is there any difference betwixt their drink, being only fresh sweet water, which the rivers yield them in great abundance.

After some little pause, our Companion (who could speak English) by our request desired to know of him something concerning their Original and how that people speaking the Language of such a remote Countrey, should come to inhabit there, having not, as we could see, any ships or Boats amongst them the means to bring them thither, and which was more, altogether ignorant and meer strangers to ships, or shipping, the main thing conducible to that means, to which request of ours, the courteous Prince thus replyed.

Friends (for so your actions declare you to be, and shall by ours find no less) know that we are inhabitants of this Island of no great standing, my Grandfather being the first that ever set foot on this shore, whose native Countrey was a place called England, far distant from this our Land, as he let us to understand; He came from that place upon the Waters, in a thing called a Ship, of which no question but you may have heard; several other persons were in his company, not intending to have come hither (as he said) but to a place called India, when tempestuous weather brought him and his company upon this Coast, where falling among the Rocks his ship split all in pieces; the whole company perishing in the Waters, saving only him and four women, which by means of a broken piece of that Ship, by Divine assistance got on Land.

What after passed (said he) during my Grandfathers life, I shall show you in a Relation thereof written by his own hand, which he delivered to my Father being his eldest Son, charging him to have a special care thereof, and ashuring him that time would bring some people or other thither to whom he would have him to impart it, that the truth of our first planting here might not be quite lost, which his commands my Father dutifully obeyed; but no one coming, he at his death delivered the same with the like charge to me, and you being the first people, which (besides our selves) ever set footing in this Island, I shall therefore in obedience to my Grandfathers and Fathers commands, willingly impart the same unto you.

Then stepping into a kind of inner room, which as we conceived was his lodging Chamber, he brought forth two sheets of paper fairly written in Englishy (being the same Relation which you had Printed with you at London) and very distinctly read the same over unto us, which we hearkened unto with great delight and admiration, freely proffering us a Copy of the same, which we afterward took and brought away along with us; which Copy hereafter followeth.[1]

1   Here begins the first part of the tract.

A Way to the East India's being lately discovered by Sea, to the South of Affrich by certain Portugals, far more safe and profitable then had been heretofore; certain English Merchants encouraged by the great advantages arising from the Eastern Commodities, to settle a Factory there for the advantage of Trade. And having to that purpose obtained the Queens Royal Licence Anno Dom. 1569. 11. or 12. Eliz. furnisht out for those parts four ships, my Master being sent as Factor to deal and Negotiate for them, and to settle there, took with him his whole Family, (that is to say) his Wife, and one Son of about twelve years of age, and one Daughter of about fourteen years, two Maidservants, one Negro female slave, and my Self, who went under him as his Book-keeper, with this company on Monday the third of April next following, (having all necessaries for Housekeeping when we should come there), we Embarqued our selves in the good ship called the India Merchant, of about four hundred and fifty Tuns burthen, and having a good wind, we on the fourteenth day of May had sight of the Canaries, and not long after of the Isles of Cafe Vert or Verd, where taking in such things as were necessary for our Voyage, and some fresh Provisions, we stearing our course South, and a point East, about the first of August came within sight of the Island of St Hellen, where we took in some fresh water, we then set our faces for the Cape of Good Hope, where by Gods blessing after some sickness, whereof some of our company died, though none of our family; and hitherto we had met with none but calm weather, yet so it pleased God, when we were almost in fight of St. Laurence, an

Island so called, one of the greatest in the world, as Marriners say, we were overtaken and dispersed by a great storm of Wind, which continued with luch violence many days, that losing all hope of safety, being out of our own knowledge, and whether we should fall on Flats or Rocks, uncertain in the nights, not having the least benefit of the light, we feared most, alwayes wishing for day, and then for Land, but it came too soon for our good; for about the first of October, our fears having made us forget how the time passed to a certainty; we about the break of day discerned Land (but what we knew not) the Land seemed high and Rockey, and the Sea continued still very stormy and tempestuous, insomuch as there seemed no hope of safety, but looked suddenly to perish. As we grew near Land, perceiving no safety in the ship, which we looked would suddenly be beat in pieces: The Captain, my Master, and some others got into the long Boat, thinking by that means to save their lives, and presently after all the Seamen cast themselves overboard, thinking to save their lives by swimming, onely myself my Masters Daughters, the two Maids, and the Negro were left on board, for we could not swim; but those that left us, might as well have tarried with us, for we saw them, or most of them perish, our selves now ready after to follow their fortune, but God was pleased to spare our lives, as it were by miracle, though to further sorrow; for when we came against the Rocks, our ship having endured two or three blows against the Rocks, (being now broken and quite foundred in the Waters), we having with much ado gotten our selves on the Bowspright, which being broken off, was driven by the Waves into a small Creek, wherein fell a little River, which being encompassed by the Rocks was sheltered from the Wind, so that we had opportunity to land our selves, (though almost drowned) in all four persons, besides the Negro: when we were got upon the Rock, we could perceive the miserable Wrack to our great terrour, I had in my pocket a little Tinder-box, and Steel, and Flint to strike fire at any time upon occasion, which served now to good Purpose, for its being so close, preserved the Tinder dry, with this, and the help of some old rotten Wood which we got together, we kindled a fire and dryed our selves, which done, I left my female company, and went to see, if I could find any of our Ships company, that were escaped, but could hear of none, though I hooted, and made all the noise I could; neither could I perceive the foot-steps of any living

Creature (save a few Birds, and other Fowls). At length it drawing towards the Evening, I went back to my company, who were very much troubled for want of me. I being now all their stay in this lost condition, we were at first afraid that the wild people of the Countrey might find us out, although we saw no footsteps of any, not so much as a Path; the Woods round about being full of Briers and Brambles, we also stood in fear of wild Beasts, of such also we saw none, nor sign of any: But above all, and that we had greatest reason to fear, was to be starved to death for want of Food, but God had otherwise provided for us, as you shall know hereafter; this done, we spent our time in getting some broken pieces of Boards, and Planks, and some of the Sails and Rigging on shore for shelter; I set up two or three Poles, and drew two or three of the Cords and Lines from Tree to Tree, over which throwing some Sail-cloathes, and having gotten Wood by us, and three or four Sea-gowns, which we had dryed, we took up our Lodging for that night altogether (the Blackmoor being left sensible then the rest we made our Centry) we slept soundly that night, as having not slept in three or four nights before (our fears of what happened preventing us) neither could our hard lodging, fear, and danger hinder us we were so over wacht.

On the morrow, being well refresht with sleep, the winde ceased, and the weather was very warm; we went down the Rocks on the sands at low water, where we found great part of our lading, either on shore or floating near it. I by the help of my company, dragged most of it on shore; what was too heavy for us broke, and we unbound the Casks and Cherts, and, taking out the goods, secured all; so that we wanted no clothes, nor any other provision necessary for Housekeeping, to furnish a better house than any we were like to have; but no victuals (the last water having spoiled all) only one Cask of bisket, being lighter than the rest was dry; this served for bread a while, and we found on Land a sort of fowl about the bigness of a Swan, very heavie and fat, that by reason of their weight could not fly, of these we found little difficulty to kill, so that was our present food; we carried out of England certain Hens and Cocks to eat by the way, some of these when the ship was broken, by some means got to land, & bred exceedingly, so that in the future they were a great help unto us; we found also, by a little River, in the flags, store of eggs, of a sort of foul much like our Ducks, which were very good meat, so that we wanted nothing to keep us alive.

On the morrow, which was the third day, as soon as it was morning, seeing nothing to disturb us, I lookt out a convenient place to dwell in, that we might build us a Hut to shelter us from the weather, and from any other danger of annoyance, from wild beasts (if any should finde us out: So close by a large spring which rose out of a high hill over-looking the Sea, on the side of a wood, having a prospect towards the Sea) by the help of an Ax and some other implements (for we had all necessaries, the working of the Sea, having cast up most of our goods) I cut down all the straightest poles I could find, and which were enough for my purpose, by the help of my company (necessity being our Master) I digged holes in the earth setting my poles at an equl distance, and nailing the broken boards of the Caskes, Cherts, and Cabins, and such like to them, making my door to the Seaward, and having covered the top, with sail-clothes strain'd and nail'd, I in the space of a week had made a large Cabbin big enough to hold all our goods and our selves in it, I also placed our Hamocks for lodging, purposing (if it pleased God to send any Ship that way) we might be transported home, but it never came to pass, the place, wherein we were (as I conceived) being much out of the way.

We having now lived in this manner full four months, and not so much as seeing or hearing of any wild people, or of any of our own company, more then our selves (they being found now by experience to be all drowned) and the place, as we after found, being a large Island, and disjoyned, and out of fight of any other Land, was wholly uninhabited by any people, neither was there any hurtful beast to annoy us: But on the contrary the countrey so very pleasant, being always clothed with green, and full of pleasant fruits, and variety of birds, ever warm, and never colder then in England in September: So that this place (had it the culture, that skilful people might bestow on it) would prove a Paradise.

The Woods afforded us a sort of Nuts, as big as a large Apple, whose kernel being pleasant and dry, we made use of instead of bread, that fowl before mentioned, and a sort of water-fowl like Ducks, and their eggs, and a beast about the size of a Goat, and almost such a like creature, which brought two young ones at a time, and that twice a year, of which the Low Lands and Woods were very full, being a very harmless creature and tame, so that we could easily take and kill them: Fish, also, especially Shell-fish (which we could best come by) we had great store of, so that in effect as to Food we wanted nothing; and thus, and by such like helps, we continued six moneths without any disturbance or want.

Idleness and Fulness of every thing begot in me a desire of enjoying the women, beginning now to grow more familiar, I had perswaded the two Maids to let me lie with them, which I did at first in private, but after, custome taking away shame (there being none but us) we did it more openly, as our Lusts gave us liberty; afterwards my Masters Daughter was content also to do as we did; the truth is, they were all handsome Women, when they had Cloathes, and well shaped, feeding well. For we wanted no Food, and living idlely, and seeing us at Liberty to do our wills, without hope of ever returning home made us thus bold: One of the first of my Comforts with whom I first accompanined (the tallest and handsomest) proved presently with child, the second was my Masters Daughter, and the other also not long after fell into the same condition: none now remaining but my Negro, who seeing what we did, longed also for her share; one Night, I being asleep, my Negro, (with the consent of the others) got close to me, thinking it being dark, to beguile me, but I awaking and feeling her, and perceiving who it was, yet willing to try the difference, satissied my self with her, as well as with one of the rest: that night, although the first time, she proved also with child, so that in the year of our being here, all my women were with child by me, and they all coming at different seasons, were a great help to one another.

The first brought me a brave Boy, my Masters Daughter was the youngest, she brought me a Girl, so did the other Maid, who being something fat sped worse at her labour: the Negro had no pain at all, brought me a fine white Girl, so I had one Boy and three Girls, the Women were soon well again, and the two first with child again before the two last were brought to bed, my custome being not to lie with any of them after they were with child, till others were so likewise, and not with the black at all after she was with child, which commonly was at the first time I lay with her, which was in the night and not else, my stomach would not serve me, although she was one of the handsomest Blacks I had seen, and her children as comly as any of the rest; we had no clothes for them, and therefore when they had suckt, we laid them in Mosse to sleep, and took no further care of them, for we knew, when they were gone more would come, the Women never failing once a year at least, and none of the Children (for all the hardship we put them to) were ever sick; so that wanting now nothing but Cloathes, nor them much neither, other than for decency, the warmth of the Countrey and Custome supplying that Defect, we were now well satissied with our condition, our Family beginning to grow large, there being nothing to hurt us, we many times lay abroad on Mossey Banks, under the shelter of some Trees, or such like (for having nothing else to do) I had made me several Arbors to sleep in with my Women in the heat of the day, in these I and my women passed the time away, they being never willing to be out of my company.

And having now no thought of ever returning home, as having resolved and sworn each to other, never to part or leave one another, or the place; having by my several wives, forty seven Children, Boys and Girls, but most Girls, and growing up apace, we were all of us very fleshly, the Country so well agreeing with us, that we never ailed any thing; my Negro having had twelve, was the first that left bearing, so I never medled with her more: My Masters Daughter (by whom I had most children, being the youngest and handsomest) was most fond of me, and I of her. Thus we lived for sixteen years, till perceiving my eldest Boy to mind the ordinary work of Nature, by seeing what we did, I gave him a Mate, and so I did to all the rest, as fast as they grew up, and were capable: My Wives having left bearing, my children began to breed apace, so we were like to be a multitude; My first Wife brought me thirteen children, my second seven, my Masters Daughter fifteen, and the Negro twelve, in all forty seven.

After we had lived there twenty two years, my Negro died suddenly, but I could not perceive any thing that ailed her; most of my children being grown, as fast as we married them, I sent them and placed them over the River by themselves severally, because we would not pester one another; and now they being all grown up, and gone, and married after our manner (except some two or three of the youngest) for (growing my self into years) I liked not the wanton annoyance of young company.

Thus having lived to the fiftieth year of my age, and the fortieth of my coming thither, at which time I sent for all of them to bring their children, and there were in number descended from me by these four Women, of my Children, Grand-children, and great Grand-children, five hundred sixty five of both sorts, I took off the Males of one Family, and married them to the Females of another, not letting any to marry their sisters, as we did formerly out of necessity, so blessing God for his Providence and goodness, I dismist them, I having taught some of my children to read formerly, for I had left still the Bible, I charged it should be read once a moneth at a general meeting: At last one of my Wives died being sixty eight years of age, which I buried in a place, set out on purpose, and within a year after another, so I had none now left but my Masters Daughter, and we lived together twelve years longer, at length she died also, so I buried her also next the place where I purposed to be buried my self, and the tall Maid my first Wife next me on the other side, the Negro next without her, and the other Maid next my Masters Daughter. I had now nothing to mind, but the place whether I was to go, being very old, almost eighty years, I gave my Cabin and Furniture that was left to my eldest son after my decease, who had married my eldest Daughter by my beloved Wife, whom I made King and Governour of all the rest: I informed them of the Manners of Europe, and charged them to remember the Christian Religion, after the manner of them that spake the same Language, and to admit no other; if hereafter any should come and find them out.

And now once for all, I summoned them to come to me, that I might number them, which I did, and found the estimate to contain in or about the eightieth year of my age, and the fifty ninth of my coming there; in all, of all sorts, one thousand seven hundred eighty and nine. Thus praying God to multiply them, and lend them the true light of the Gospel, I last of all dismist them: For, being now very old, and my sight decayed, I could not expect to live long. I gave this Narration (written with my own hand) to my eldest Son, who now lived with me, commanding him to keep it, and if any strangers should come hither by chance, to let them see it, and take a Copy of it if they would, that our name be not lost from off the earth. I gave this people (descended from me) the name of the ENGLISH PINES, George Pine being my name, and my

Masters Daughters name Sarah English, my two other Wives were Mary Sparkes, and Elizabeth Trevor, so their severall Defendants are called the ENGLISH, the SPARKS, and the TREVORS, and the PHILLS, from the Christian Name of the Negro, which was Philippa, she having no surname: And the general name of the whole the ENGLISH PINES; vvhom God bless vvith the dew of Heaven, and the fat of the Earth, AMEN.[1]

1   Here ended the first part.

After the reading and delivering unto us a Coppy of this Relation, then proceeded he on in his discourse.

My Grandfather when he wrote this, was as you hear eighty yeares of age, there proceeding from his Loyns one thousand seven hundred eighty nine children, which he had by them four women aforesaid: My Father was his eldest son, and was named Henry, begotten of his wife Mary Sparkes, whom he apointed chief Governour and Ruler over the rest; and having given him a charge not to exercise tyranny over them, seeing they were his fellow brethren by Fathers side (of which there could be no doubt made of double dealing therein) exhorting him to use justice and sincerity amongst them, and not to let Religion die with him, but to observe and keep those Precepts which he had taught them, he quietly surrendred up his soul, and was buried with great lamentation of all his children.

My father coming to rule, and the people growing more populous, made them to range further in the discovery of the Countrey, which they found answerable to their desires, full both of Fowls and Beasts, and those too not hurtful to mankinde, as if this Country (on which we were by providence cast without arms or other weapons to defend our selves, or offend others,) should by the same providence be so inhabited as not to have any need of such like weapons of destruction wherewith to preserve our lives.

But as it is impossible, but that in multitudes disorders will grow, the stronger seeking to oppress the weaker; no tye of Religion being strong enough to chain up the depraved nature of mankinde, even so amongst them mischiefs began to rise, and they soon fell from those good orders prescribed them by my Grandfather. The source from whence those mischiefs spring, was at first, I conceive, the neglect of hearing the Bible read, which according to my Grandfathers proscription, was once a moneth at a general meeting, but now many of them wandring far up into the Country, they quite neglected the coming to it, with all other means of Christian instruction, whereby the sence of sin being quite lost in them, they fell to whoredoms, incests, and adulteries; so that what my Grandfather was forced to do for necessity, they did for wantonness; nay not confining themselves within the bound of any modesty, but brother and sister lay openly together; those who would not yield to their lewd embraces, were by force ravished, yea many times endangered of their lives. To redress those enormities, my father assembled all the Company near unto him, to whom he declared the wickedness of those their brethren; who all with one consent agreed that they should be severely punished; and so arming themselves with boughs, stones, and such like weapons, they marched against them, who having notice of their coming, and fearing their deserved punishment, some of them fled into woods, others passed over a great River, which runneth through the heart of our Countrey, hazarding drowning to escape punishment; But the grandest offender of them all was taken, whole name was John Phill, the second son of the Negro-woman that came with my Grandfather into this Island.

He being proved guilty of divers ravishings & tyrannies committed by him, was adjudged guilty of death, and accordingly was thrown down from a high Rock into the Sea, where he perished in the waters. Execution being done upon him, the rest were pardoned for what was past, which being notified abroad, they returned from those Defait and Obscure places, wherein they were hidden.

Now as Seed being cast into stinking Dung produceth good and wholesome Corn for the Indentation of mans life, so bad manners produceth good and wholesome Laws for the preservation of Humane Society. Soon after my Father with the advice of some few others of his Counsel, ordained and set forth these Laws to be observed by them.

1. That whosoever should blaspheme or talk irreverently of the name of God should be put to death.

2. That who should be absent from the monethly assembly to hear the Bible read, without sufficient cause shown to the contrary, should for the first default be kept without any victuals or drink, for the space of four days, and if he offend therein again, then to suffer death.
3. That who should force or ravish any Maid or Woman should be burnt to death, the party so ravished putting fire to the wood that should burn him.
4. Whosoever shall commit adultery, for the first crime the Male shall lose his Privities, and the Woman have her right eye bored out, if after that she was again taken in the act, she should die without mercy.
5. That who so injured his Neighbour, by laming of his Limbs, or taking any thing away which he possesseth, shall suffer in the same kind himself by loss of Limb; and for defrauding his Neighbour, to become servant to him, whilst he had made him double satisfaction.
6. That, who should defame or speak evil of the Governour, or refuse to come before him upon Summons, should receive a punishment by whipping with Rods, and afterwards be exploded from the society of the rest of the inhabitants.

Having set forth these Laws, he chose four several persons under him to see them put in Execution, whereof one was of the Englishes, the Off-spring of Sarah English; another of his own Tribe, the Sparks; a third of the Trevors, and the fourth of the Phills, appointing them every year at a certain time to appear before him, and give an account of what they had done in the prosecution of those Laws.

The Countrey being thus settled, my father lived quiet and peaceable till he attained to the age of ninety and four years, when dying, I succeeded in his place, in which I have continued peaceably and quietly till this very present time.

He having ended his Speech, we gave him very heartily thanks for our information, assuring him we should not be wanting to him in any thing which lay in our powers, wherewith we could pleasure him in what he should desire, and thereupon preferred to depart, but before our going away, he would needs engage us to see him, the next day, when was to be their great assembly or monethly meeting for the celebration of their Religious Exercises.

Accordingly the next day we came thither again, and were courteously entertained as before, In a short space there was gathered such a multitude of people together as made us to admire; and first there were several Weddings celebrated, the manner whereof was thus. The Bridegroom and Bride appeared before him who was their Priest or Reader of the Bible, together with the Parents of each party, or if any of their Parents were dead, then the next relation unto them, without whose consent as well as the parties to be married, the Priest will not joyn them together; but being satissied in those particulars, after some short Oraizons, and joyning of hands together, he pronounces them to be man and wife: and with exhortations to them to live lovingly towards each other, and quietly towards their neighbors, he concludes with some prayers, and so dismisses them.

The Weddings being finished, all the people took their places to hear the Word read, the new married persons having the honour to be next unto the Priest that day, after he had read three or four Chapters he fell to expounding the most difficult places therein, the people being very attentive all that while, this exercise continued for two or three hours, which being done, with some few prayers he concluded, but all the rest of that day was by the people kept very strictly, abstaining from all manner of playing or pastimes, with which on other dayes they use to pass their time away, as having need of nothing but victuals, and that they have in such plenty as almost provided to their hands.

Their exercises of Religion being over, we returned again to our Ship, and the next day, taking with us two or three Fowling-pieces leaving half our Company to guard the Ship, the rest of us resolved to go up higher into the Country for a further discovery: All the way as we passed the first morning, we saw abundance of little Cabbins or Huts of these inhabitants, made under Trees, and fashioned up with boughs, grass, and such like stuffe to defend them from the Sun and Rain; and as we went along, they came out of them much wondering at our Attire, and standing aloof off from us as if they were afraid, but our companion that spake English, calling to them in their own Tongue, and giving them good words, they drew nigher, some of them freely proffering to go along with us, which we willingly accepted; but having passed some few miles, one of our company espying a Beast like unto a Goat come gazing on him, he discharged his Peece, sending a brace of Bullets into his belly, which brought him dead upon the ground; these poor naked unarmed people hearing the noise of the Peece, and seeing the Beast lie tumbling in his gore, without speaking any words betook them to their heels, running back again as fast as they could drive, nor could the perswasions of our Company, assuring them they should have no hurt, prevail anything at all with them, so that we were forced to pass along without their company: all the way that we went we heard the delightful harmony of singing Birds, the ground very fertile in Trees, Grass, and such flowers, as grow by the production of Nature, without the help of Art; many and several sorts of Beads we saw, who were not so much wild as in other Countries; whether it were as having enough to satiate themselves without ravening upon others, or that they never before saw the sight of man, nor heard the report of murdering Guns, I leave it to others to determine. Some Trees bearing wild Fruits we also saw, and of those some whereof we tailed, which were neither unwholsome nor distasteful to the Pallate, and no question had but Nature here the benefit of Art added unto it, it would equal, if not exceed many of our European Countries; the Vallyes were every where intermixt with running streams, and no question but the earth hath in it rich veins of Minerals, enough to satisfie the desires of the most covetous.

It was very strange to us, to see that in such a fertile Countrey which was as yet never inhabited, there should be notwithstanding such a free and clear passage to us, without the hinderance of Bushes, Thorns, and such like fluff, wherewith most Islands of the like nature are pestered: the length of the Grass (which yet was very much intermixt with flowers) being the only impediment that we found.

Six dayes together did we thus travel, setting several marks in our way as we went for our better return, not knowing whether we should have the benefit of the Stars for our guidance in our going back, which we made use of in our passage: at last we came to the vast Ocean on the other side of the Island, and by our coasting it, conceive it to be of an oval form, only here and there shooting forth with some Promontories. I conceive it hath but few good

Harbours belonging to it, the Rocks in most places making it inaccessible. The length of it may be about two hundred, and the breadth one hundred miles, the whole in circumference about five hundred miles.

It lyeth about seventy six degrees of Longitude, and twenty of Latitude, being scituate under the third Climate, the longest day being about thirteen hours and fourty five minutes. The weather, as in all Southern Countries, is far more hot than with us in Europe; but what is by the Sun parched in the day, the night again refreshes with cool pearly dews. The Air is found to be very healthful by the long lives of the present inhabitants, few dying there till such time as they come to good years of maturity, many of them arriving to the extremity of old age.

And now speaking concerning the length of their Lives, I think it will not be amisse in this place to speak something of their Burials, which they used to do thus.

When the party was dead, they stuck his Carkass all over with flowers, and after carried him to the place appointed for Burial, where setting him down, (the Priest having given some godly Exhortations concerning the frailty of life) then do they take stones (a heap being provided there for that purpose) and the nearest of the kin begins to lay the first stone upon him, afterwards the rest follows, they never leaving till they have covered the body deep in stones, so that no Beast can possibly come to him, and this first were they forced to make, having no Spades or Shovels wherewith to dig them Graves; which want of theirs we espying, bestowed a Pick-ax and two Shovels upon them.

Here might I add their way of Christening Children, but that being little different from yours in ENGLAND, and taught them by GEORGE PINES at first which they have since continued, I shall therefore forbear to speak thereof.

After our return back from the discovery of the Countrey, the Wind not being fit for our purpose, and our men also willing thereto, we got all our cutting Instruments on Land, and fell to hewing down of Trees, with which, in a little time,(many hands making light work) we built up a Pallace for this William Pines the Lord of that Countrey; which, though much inferiour to the houses of your Gentry in England. Yet to them which never had seen better, it appeared a very Lordly Place. This deed of ours was beyond expression acceptable unto him, load-ing us with thanks for so great a benefit, of which he said he should never be able to make a requital.

And now acquainting him, that upon the first opportunity we were resolved to leave the Island, as also how that we were near Neighbours to the Countrey of England, from whence his Ancestors came; he seemed upon the news to be much discontented that we would leave him, desiring, if it might stand with our commodity to continue still with him, but seeing he could not prevail, he invited us to dine with him the next day, which we promised to do, against which time he provided, very sumptuously (according to his estate) for us, and now was he attended after a more Royal manner than ever we saw him before, both for number of Servants, and multiplicity of Meat, on which we fed very heartily; but he having no other Beverage for us to drink, then water, we fetched from our Ship a Case of Brandy, presenting some of it to him to drink, but when he had tasted of it, he would by no means be perswaded to touch thereof again, preferring (as he said) his own Countrey Water before all such Liquors whatsoever.

After we had Dined, we were invited out into the Fields to behold their Country Dauncing, which they did with great agility of body; and though they had no other then only Vocal Musick (several of them singing all that while) yet did they trip it very neatly, giving sufficient satisfaction to all that beheld them.

The next day we invited the Prince William Pines aboard our Ship, where was nothing wanting in what we could to entertain him, he had about a dozen of Servants to attend on him he much admired at the Tacklings of our Ship, but when we came to discharge a piece or two of Ordnance, it struck him into a wonder and amazement to behold the strange effects of Powder; he was very sparing in his Diet, neither could he, or any of his followers be induced to drink any thing but Water: We there presented him with several things, as much as we could spare, which we thought would any wayes conduce to their benefit, all which he very gratefully received, assuring us of his real love and good will, whensoever we should come thither again.

And now we intended the next day to take our leaves, the Wind standing fair, blowing with a gentle Gale South and by East, but as we were hoisting of our Sails, and weighing Anchor, we were suddenly Allarm'd with a noise from the shore, the Prince, W. Pines imploring our assistance in an Insurection which had happened amongst them, of which this was the cause.

Henry Phil, the chief Ruler of the Tribe or Family of the Phils, being the Offspring of George Pines which he had by the Negro-woman; this man had ravished the Wife of one of the principal of the Family of the Trevors, which act being made known, the Trevors assembled themselves all together to bring the offender unto Justice: But he knowing his crime to be so great, as extended to the loss of life: fought to defend that by force, which he had as unlawfully committed, whereupon the whole Island was in a great hurly burly, they being too great Potent Factions, the bandying of which against each other, threatned a general ruin to the whole State.

The Governour William Pines had interposed in the matter, but found his Authority too weak to repress such Disorders; for where the Hedge of Government is once broken down, the most vile bear the greatest rule, whereupon he desired our assistance, to which we readily condescended, and arming out twelve of us went on Shore, rather as to a surprize than fight, for what could nakedness do to encounter with Arms. Being conducted by him to the force of our Enemy, we first entered into parley, seeking to gain them rather by fair means then force, but that not prevailing, we were necesitated to use violence, for this Henry Phill being of an undaunted resolution, and having armed his fellows with Clubs and Stones, they sent such a Peal amongst us, as made us at the first to give back, which encouraged them to follow us on with great violence, but we discharging off three or four Guns, when they saw some of themselves wounded, and heard the terrible reports which they gave, they ran away with greater speed then they came. The Band of the Trevors who were joyned with us, hotly pursued them, and having taken their Captain, returned with great triumph to their Governour, who fitting in Judgment upon him, he was adjudged to death, and thrown off a steep Rock into the Sea, the only way they have of punishing any by death, except burning.

And now at last we took our solemn leaves of the Governour, and departed from thence, having been there in all, the space of three weeks and two dayes, we took with us good store of the flesh of a Beast which they call there Reval, being in taste different either from Beef or Swines-flesh, yet very delightful to the Pallate, and exceeding nutrimental. We took also with us alive, divers Fowls which they call Marde, about the bigness of a Pullet, and not different in taste, they are very swift of flight, and yet so fearless of danger, that they will stand still till such time as you catch them: We had also sent us in by the Governour about two bushels of eggs, which as I conjecture were the Mards eggs, very lusious in taste, and strenthening to the body.

June 8. We had a sight of Cambaia, a part of the East Indies, but; under the Government of the great Cham of Tartary here our Vessel springing a leak, we were forced to put to Chore, receiving much dammage in some of our Commodities; we were forced to ply the Pump for eighteen hours together, which, had that miscarried, we had inevitably have perished; here we stai'd five dayes mending our Ship, and drying some of our Goodss and then hoisting Sail, in four days time more we came to Calecute.

This Calecute is the chief Mart Town and Staple of all the Indian Traffique, it is very populous, and frequented by Merchants of all Nations. Here we unladed a great part of our Goods, and taking in others, which caused us to stay there a full Moneth, during which space, at leisure times I went abroad to take a survey of the City, which I found to be large and populous, lying for three miles together upon the Sea-shore. Here is a great many of those persons whom thy call Brackmans, being their Priests or Teachers whom they much reverence. It is a custome here for the King to give to some of those Brachmain, the handelling of his Nuptial Bed; for which cause, not the Kings, but the Kings sisters sons succeed in the Kingdom, as being more certainly known to be of the true Royal blood: And these sisters of his choose what Gentleman they please on whom to bestow their Virginities; and if they prove not in a certain time to be with child, they betake themselves to these Brachman Stalions, who never fail of doing their work.

The people are indifferently civil and ingenious, both men and women imitate a Majesty in their Train and Apparel, which they sweeten, with Oyles and Perfumes: adorning themselves with Jewels and other Ornaments befitting each Rank and Quality of them.

They have many odd Customs amongst them which they observe very strictly; as first, not knowing their Wives after they have born them two children: Secondly, not accompanying them, if after five years cohabition they can raise no issue by them, but taking others in their rooms: Thirdly, never being rewarded for any Military exploit, unless they bring with them an enemies Head in their Hand, but that which is strangest, and indeed most barbarous, is that when any of their friends falls sick, they will rather chuse to kill him, then that he should be withered by sickness.

Thus you see there is little employment there for Doctors, when to be sick, is the next wan for to be slain, or perhaps the people may be of the mind rather to kill themselves, then to let the Doctors do it.

Having dispatched our business, and sraighted again our Ship, we left Calecute, and put forth to Sea, and coasted along several of the Islands belonging to India, at Camboia I met with our old friend Mr. David Prire, who was overjoyed to see me, to whom I related our Discovery of the Island of Pines, in the same manner as I have related it to you; he was then but newly recovered of a Feaver, the Air of that place not being agreeable to him; here we took in good store of Aloes, and some other Commodities, and victualled our Ship for our return home.

After four dayes failing we met with two Portugal Ships which came from Lisbon, one whereof had in a storm lost its Top-mast, and was forced in part to be towed by the other. We had no bad weather in eleven dayes space, but then a sudden storm of Wind did us much harm in our Tacklings, and swept away one of our Sailors off from the Fore Castle. November the sixth had like to have been a fatal day unto us, our Ship striking twice upon a Rock, and at night was in danger of being fired by the negligence of a Boy, leaving a Candle carelesly in the Gun-room; the next day we were chafed by a Pyrate Argiere, but by the swiftness of our Sails we out ran him. December the first we came again to Madagascar, where we put in for a fresh recruit of Victuals and Water.

During our abode here, there hapned a very great Earthquake, which tumbled down many Houses; The people of themselves are very Unhospitable and Treacherous, hardly to to be drawn to Traffique with any people; and now, this calamitie happening upon them, so enraged them against the Christians, imputing all luch calamities to the cause of them, that they fell upon some Portugais and wounded them, and we seeing their mischievous Actions, with all the speed we could put forth to Sea again, and sailed to the Island of St. Hellens.

Here we stayed all the Chrismas Holy-dayes, which was vere much celebrated by the Governour there under the King of Spain. Here we furnished ourselves with all necessaries which we wanted; but upon our departure, our old acquaintance Mr. Petrus Ramazina, coming in a Skiff out of the Isle del Principe, or the Princes Island, retarded our going for the space of two dayes, for both my self and our Purser had Emergent business with him, he being concerned in those Affairs of which I wrote to you in April last: Indeed we cannot but acknowledge his Courtesies unto us, of which you know he is never sparing. January the first, we again hoisted Sail, having a fair and prosperous gail of Wind, we touched at the Canaries, but made no tarriance, desirous now to see our Native Countrey; but the Winds was very cross unto us for the space of a week, at last we were savoured with a gentle Gale, which brought us on merrily; though we were on a sudden stricken again into a dump; a Sailor from the main Mast discovering five Ships, which put us all in a great fear, we being Richly Laden, and not very well provided for Defence; but they bearing up to us, we found them to be Zealanders and our Friends; after many other passages concerning us, not so much worthy of Note, we at last safele arrived at home, May 26. 1668.

Thus Sir, have I given you a brief, but true Relation of our Voyage, Which I was the more willing to do, to prevent false Copies which might be spread of this nature: As for the Island of Pines it self, which caused me to Write this Relation, I suppose it is a thing so strange as will hardly be credited by some, although perhaps knowing persons, especially considering our last age being so full of Discoveries, that this Place should lie Dormant for so long a space of time; Others I know, such.

Nullifidians as will believe nothing but what they see, applying that Proverb unto us, That travelers may lye by authority. But Sir, in writing to you, I question not but to give Credence, you knowing my disposition so hateful to divulge Falsities; I shall request you to impart this my Relation to Mr. W. W. and Mr. P. L. remembring me very kindly unto them, not forgetting my old acquaintance, Mr. J. P.

and Mr. J. B. no more at present, but only my best respects to you and your second self I rest,

Yours in the best of friendship,
Henry Cornelius Fan Sloetten.
July 22. 1668.

POST-SCRIPT:

ONE thing concerning the Isle of Pines, I had almost quite forgot, we had with us an Irish man named Dermot Conelly who had formerly been in England, and had learned there to play on the Bag-pipes, which he carried to Sea with him; yet so un-Englished he was, that he had quite forgotten your Language, but still retained his Art of Bagpipe-playing, in which he took extraordinary delight; being one day on Land in the Isle of Pines, he played on them, but to see the admiration of those naked people concerning them, would have striken you into admiration; long time it was before we could perswade them that it was not a living creature, although they were permitted to touch and feel it, and yet are the people very intelligible, retaining a great part of the Ingenuity and Gallantry of the English Nation, though they have not that happy means to express themselves; in this respect we may account them fortunate, in that possessing little, they enjoy all things, as being contented with what they have, wanting those alurements to mischief, which our European Countries are enriched with. I shall not dilate any further, no question but time will make this Island known better to the world; all that I shall ever say of it is, that it is a place enriched with Natures abundance, deficient in nothing conducible to the sustentation of mans life, which were it Manured by Agriculture and Gardening, as other of our European Countries are, no question but it would equal, if not exceed many which now pass for praiseworthy.

FINIS.

LaVergne, TN USA
14 September 2009
157830LV00002B/100/P